HIDDEN HISTORY
of
EAU CLAIRE

HIDDEN HISTORY

of

EAU CLAIRE

Diana Peterson and Jodi Kiffmeyer

THE
History
PRESS

Published by The History Press
Charleston, SC
www.historypress.com

Copyright © 2025 by Diana Peterson and Jodi Kiffmeyer
All rights reserved

Front cover: Barstow Street in downtown Eau Claire, circa 1914–21. *Courtesy Chippewa Valley Museum.*

First published 2025

Manufactured in the United States

ISBN 9781467157193

Library of Congress Control Number: 2024944882

CONTENTS

ACKNOWLEDGEMENTS

We are thankful to the Chippewa Valley Museum for bringing us together and encouraging us to pursue our love of learning about Eau Claire.

We appreciate Jarrod Showalter, our friend and former colleague, for vetting our manuscript to keep us accurate and prevent typos and other "unplanned occurrences" from sneaking into our book.

Diana is grateful for her family, who are often called on for feedback on her writing drafts and never complain no matter how often they hear, "I'll be there as soon as I finish this paragraph."

Jodi thanks her grandmothers for fostering and sustaining her love of local history. Thanks to Grandma Irene for starting me out on old family stories as a toddler sitting with her in her special chair. And thanks to Grandma Bev for keeping me motivated by listening to my stories from her special chair 1,500 miles away.

And a big shout-out of thanks to our readers for helping us to preserve the past of Eau Claire.

—Jodi and Diana

PREFACE

W e grew up enveloped in an appreciation of history. Jodi had two grandmothers who fostered and sustained her love of local history by sharing family stories with her when she was a toddler and throughout her lifetime. Diana grew up in Pennsylvania, where family houses going back to the 1750s still stood. Her grandmothers also knew the importance of passing on family stories.

Eventually, we made our way to the Chippewa Valley Museum, where Jodi is archivist and Diana is editor. While researching exhibits and writing social media posts, we often run across little story seeds. There's often not enough time to let these stories develop without neglecting the other important parts of our jobs.

Hidden History of Eau Claire gave us the opportunity to cultivate a few dozen of those stories in our personal time. Most of these accounts will be new to Eau Clairians. Some of them are better known, and we have tried to delve deeper into those to provide new information. Some of the stories are full of humor; some are heartbreaking. Some feature people well-known in the community and, sometimes, in the nation, while others are about residents who quietly went about their daily lives. Some of the characters had families who lived in Eau Claire for generations, while others were here for a short time before moving on.

All these people had a unique perspective and an important story to tell. They each represent a root securing today's Eau Claire to its rich past. Perhaps the book will inspire some of you to discover, document and share your own family stories. We hope that you find these individuals as fascinating as we do.

Happy reading.

—Diana and Jodi

PART I

MURDER, MYSTERY AND MAYHEM

Chapter 1

MRS. TOUSLEY'S BODY

by Jodi Kiffmeyer

No one knew where to bury Mrs. Tousley's body, but that was the least of her problems.

Late in February 1903, an article titled "Mrs. Tousley" appeared in the *Eau Claire Weekly Telegram*, a mysterious letter signed by a woman named Isabella Horton. She addressed her message to a woman in town who'd done business with Deaconess Home in Chicago in the past. The subject was the remains of Mrs. Ella Tousley, who died at the Home on February 16. The request was odd: Mrs. Tousley's body was on its way to Eau Claire from Chicago, and would someone please arrange to pick it up and bury it?

The writer admitted she only contacted Eau Claire because she'd heard Ella mention her mother was buried there. Though the deceased had made many friends at the Deaconess Home during the two and a half years she lived there, she'd kept silent about her life's history. When she died of a heart attack, no one at the Home was sure what to do with her body.

Eau Claire's collective memory was fuzzy at first, but eventually several people remembered Mrs. Tousley, whom they first knew as Ella Burlingham. C.L. James, a former city council member, offered what information he had in a *Weekly Telegram* letter to the editor. James figured Mrs. Tousley was a native of Eau Claire. She had two brothers. She'd attended the Methodist Episcopalian seminary in town. Her father had died around Memorial Day 1868. She married a "stranger" named Tousley, but they weren't together for long. Finally, she was well-known on the West Side of Eau Claire and "universally esteemed for intelligence, industry, modesty and discretion at a period of misfortune."

Mr. James got some things right, but Ella wasn't a native of Eau Claire. She was born in New York State around 1855, the youngest of the three children of Squire and Mary Burlingham. Ella's older siblings were indeed brothers: Pardon and Willman (later known as William). Sometime between 1860 and 1868, they all moved to Eau Claire, where Squire died on May 30, 1868. If Ella attended the Methodist Episcopal Seminary, we have no record of it.

Ella married Jason Tousley on January 31, 1875, in Omaha, Nebraska. Tousley may have been a stranger to C.L. James, but Ella knew him as her first cousin—their mothers were sisters. That marriage lasted at most a few years. Jason was married to another woman by 1879, and Ella moved back to Eau Claire before 1882. She took up dressmaking from her home as a way of supporting herself and her aging mother, Mary.

On January 19, 1898, the Eau Claire *Daily Telegram* printed a story—out of the blue—describing the pitiful situation of Mary Burlingham, who'd been waiting months for word from her daughter. It seems Ella Tousley had traveled to Minneapolis the previous fall, leaving her mother in the care of a woman who lived with them and promising to return soon. However, it was months before they heard from her. When the news came, it was unexpected. Ella was in an asylum in Spokane, Washington, imprisoned there since being declared legally insane.

What in the world was Ella doing 1,400 miles from where she was supposed to be, in Minneapolis, and how did she end up committed against her will? In the words of an Eau Claire newspaper reporter, it was because she tried to "protect, as she supposed, the interests of her dead friend."

Ella's friend was Maud Meservey. In 1897, Maud was working as a stenographer for the Montana State Board of Pardons, until an illness in June forced her to return to her father's house in Spokane. She died just weeks later, on Independence Day. The residents of Spokane helped Mr. Meservey bury the body and began to move on. Then, a mysterious Mrs. J.S. Van Atta appeared in town and challenged the facts of Maud's death.

Mrs. Van Atta claimed to be representing Maud's mother, Mary Cooper of Eau Claire, who was convinced her daughter was still alive and being held captive by someone for some reason. You can hear the bafflement of the *Spokane Chronicle* reporter, who explained that Mrs. Van Atta admitted to the chief of police that her real name was Ella Tousley but refused to offer any other details about herself or her mission. She gave no reason for

Ella Burlingame Tousley with her brothers. *Courtesy fmlyhstryldy (descendant)*.

her strong belief that Maud remained alive, and Spokane residents were at a loss to convince her otherwise.

After five weeks of it, they gave up and did what communities often did back then when faced with an intractable woman—they brought Ella to court to have her declared insane. The complaint alleged that although she was "quiet and ladylike," Ella continued to insist without proof that Maud's death was a hoax. A few days before the trial, Ella took to her bed at the Hotel Spokane and refused to eat. She became violent whenever staff approached her room. The manager felt his only choice was to let the justice system take care of her. When Ella refused to answer any of Judge Richardson's questions, he let the asylum at Medical Lake take care of her. They sent a telegram to Eau Claire, and finally, Mrs. Burlingham knew the whereabouts of her daughter.

There wasn't any real question about the certainty of Maude's death. Why did Ella have such strong convictions to the contrary? After spending two months in the asylum, she was released, on February 8, 1898. Rather than leaving for Wisconsin, she remained in Spokane to bring a lawsuit against the Hotel Spokane's owners and manager for their part in her incarceration. In the meantime, she wrote letters to the Eau Claire newspaper trying to squelch rumors about her sanity and how she came to be out West in the first place.

One of the rumors goes like this: Ella was a spiritualist whose beliefs prompted her to travel to Chicago to consult a medium when she heard news of Maud's death. In a séance, a spirit told Ella that Maud was still alive and being held captive by the speaker of the house of the State of Washington. He had fallen in love with her. Supposedly, this was the reason she wouldn't believe her friend had died. Ella wrote a letter to the *Eau Claire Leader*, published on April 7, 1898, in which she vehemently denied ever using the services of a medium and claimed she hadn't been to Chicago anytime in the previous year. She offered no explanation for her belief that Maud was being held hostage and ended her letter with the statement, "He that is without sin let him cast the first stone."

A year after her release from Medical Lake, Ella was still in Spokane trying to recover $75,000 from the hotel when the *Leader* published news of her mother's death. Mother and daughter probably hadn't seen each other since the fall 1897. After that, Mary and Ella Tousley disappeared from Eau Claire's memory until the mysterious letter from Isabella Horton arrived from Chicago four years later.

With prompting from C.L. James's letter to the editor, Eau Claire began to recall Ella. People hunted down one of her brothers, who refused to pay for or even attend a funeral because he and his sister were estranged over a financial argument. With all family options exhausted, it looked like Ella would be buried as a pauper in the potter's field. But the good people of Eau Claire decided to do the decent thing. Mrs. George W. Robinson, who had used Ella's dressmaking services in the past, offered to pay for a Christian burial. Several other society ladies joined in by lending carriages for mourners, paying for flowers and attending the funeral themselves. They laid Mrs. Tousley to rest in Lakeview Cemetery to be forgotten for another 120 years, until a curious archivist stumbled on the news of her body's impending arrival in Eau Claire.

Chapter 2
A GORY DEATH

by Diana Peterson

According to the *Weekly Leader*, the fall weather was mild and pleasant in 1891. October 9 was a beautiful evening for a walk. Mary Russell and Irene Heimbaugh left a ladies' mission meeting at Lake Street Methodist Church, where Mary's husband, Reverend Edward Russell, was pastor. The two women probably strolled over the Grand Avenue Bridge as they made their way toward their residences at 909 South Barstow and 912 South Farwell, respectively.

They had some time on their trek to discuss a few topics. Perhaps they were talking about the big hosiery sale going on at Kepler & Co. They might have had a few choice words for John Bell, who'd been quoted in the *Weekly Leader* as saying, "Women can't improve politics by getting in them." Perhaps they were sharing their opinion on Dr. G.W. Pickins bringing in Dr. D.J. Stanbury, a spiritual medium, who would be in Eau Claire for a week to give sittings for individual slate writing, Ouija board messages and other spiritual phenomena. Slate writing took place around a table during a séance. If participants heard a scratching sound, they usually found the slate covered with a message from the spirit world.

As the women made their way through Wilson Park, six blocks from the Russell home, one thing they were not thinking about in the least was where to run as they looked up just in time to see an infuriated bull charging toward them.

Frank Dick, an employee of New Brunswick farmer William Swift, was bringing a herd of cattle through town when the bull took off. As Dick raced

Burial spot for the Reverend Edward and Mary Russell, Block 13, Forest Hill Cemetery. Mary was buried in 1891, Edward in 1896. *Courtesy Diana Peterson.*

toward the women, the bull tossed Mrs. Heimbaugh ten feet and began stomping on her, leaving her bruised and bloody. The bull then went after Mrs. Russell. Dick reached them in time to beat the bull with a heavy club, sustaining many bruises and injuries himself as he fought with the wild animal.

Mrs. Heimbaugh seemed to be in a better condition than Mrs. Russell. Dick scooped Mary Russell up, carrying her to the nearest home. She was in severe pain; the bull had gored her badly, tearing her flesh. On examining her, the doctor suspected severe internal injuries.

A week later, Mary passed away at age fifty-three. The funeral was held at her home, and Mary was buried in Forest Hill Cemetery. Her husband, Edward, was a widower for the second time.

Edward had an interesting life, one that might have been typical for someone in that era. He was born in Connecticut in 1822. His family moved to Erie, Pennsylvania, where Edward lived from 1825 to 1847. His father was an active abolitionist, and Edward aided many people who escaped slavery.

Continuing his voyage westward, Edward enrolled at the Grand River Institute in Austinburg, Ohio. After graduation, he came to Wisconsin as part of a surveyor's party to explore the St. Croix area. In 1851, he became a Methodist and felt a call to preach, although his family had a bad opinion of Methodists. Despite their misgivings, he was ordained as a minister in Wisconsin in 1854.

Edward married Mary Woods from Springfield, Illinois, in 1853. She passed away in 1855 at age twenty-three and was buried in Darlington, Wisconsin. Her infant son, Thomas, must have been raised by friends or family because he remained in Darlington his entire life, marrying and having a family of his own. He was a renowned woodworker there and died from blood poisoning at age forty in 1894. His father returned to Darlington for his funeral, and Thomas was buried next to his mother.

Both of Edward's wives grew up in Springfield, Illinois, so perhaps they were related or friends. Mary Coble and Edward married in 1857, and they had five children together; their daughter Lois was a district organizer of the Woman's Christian Temperance Union. After Mary's death, Edward moved to Great Falls, Montana, to live with his son, who was a stenographer. He filled in for pastors in that area when needed. However, when he died from a stroke in 1896, his body was brought back to Eau Claire. He is also buried at Forest Hills Cemetery.

Many Eau Claire residents died downtown under weird circumstances, but a charging bull is one of the strangest.

Chapter 3
TILL DEATH DON'T US PART

by Diana Peterson

Oliver J. Chatterton was not a dependable man. The fact that he never took responsibility or followed through on his promises is what saved his wife's life in 1930.

We can make a pretty good guess about what happened to destroy the marital bliss of Burdette and Oliver Chatterton, who were living in Eau Claire in 1930. All we know for sure is that he was a shoe salesman and had just lost his job in Eau Claire. The corporation he worked for had gone through some stock shifts, so personnel were being shuffled. His manager was moving him back to Madison to one of the company's shoe stores there, so he was not losing his source of income. The couple had been married for two years—not very happily.

However, Oliver convinced Burdette to participate in a plan to do away with themselves. They rented a car and drove it to Big Falls on March 19, 1930. Burdette said she went along with his scheme, assuming he would not be able to carry it out. She said domestic troubles and quarrels led him to devise a plan to shoot Burdette and then shoot himself.

Oliver and Burdette wrote notes to leave at the scene. His said, "Burdette and I love each other. That is why we are doing this. I've been a cheat. Now I'm going to pay up." Hers said, "Dear Mother and All, forgive us but this was the only way out. We want to be buried side by side. Bud and Burdette."

You have to wonder how someone who loved his wife could have thought she should pay part of the price for his sins. When it came time to pull the trigger and shoot her as she was sitting on his lap, he lost his nerve, but he

Big Falls, the park where Oliver Chatterton chose to end his and his wife's lives. *Courtesy Chippewa Valley Museum.*

did turn the gun on himself and shoot. The bullet passed behind his right eye and lodged in the left bone cavity.

I'm guessing Burdette did not drive, because she helped Oliver walk two miles to a farmhouse, where they obtained medical care. Both of their mothers were called to travel from Madison to the hospital. Oliver was twenty-six, and Burdette was twenty-two. Oliver remained in the hospital until April 8, when he was cleared to leave Eau Claire. He lost sight in one eye, but doctors were hopeful it might return at some point.

When they returned to Madison, Oliver fell back into making the same poor choices. In 1932, Burdette obtained a divorce, claiming he was running around with other women and had not supported her financially for a year and a half. She took back her maiden name, Williams.

It was not Oliver's first marriage. In 1922, he convinced Frances Cook to elope with him in a "borrowed" Studebaker. They were later escorted back home by the police, and she obtained a divorce in 1926.

In 1934, both Oliver and Burdette wed new partners. Oliver told his wife, Victoria, that he only married her because they had been drinking heavily and that he did not love her. She filed for divorce soon after.

Happily, Burdette had a better life. She married Paul Collins, a University of Wisconsin–Madison graduate, and for a while, they lived in a cottage on Lake Mendota. At some point, they moved to Oak Ridge, Tennessee, where he opened Collins Real Estate. It was a very successful business and a very successful marriage, producing two daughters and six grandchildren. Paul passed away there in 1970, and Burdette continued to live in Oak Ridge until her death in 1984.

Oliver died in 1958 from pulmonary edema and congestion. He was still selling shoes and living in a hotel in Rockford, Illinois.

Chapter 4

A WOMAN SCORNED: HARRIET BUTCHER

by Diana Peterson

Hell hath no fury like a woman scorned. Harriet Butcher displayed that sentiment in 1930 when she was arrested for the armed assault of Sigurd Lind.

Sigurd Lind was born in Eau Claire in 1897. His father, Oluf Lind, was a profitable grocer in the city for thirty-five years. In 1920, Sigurd and his brother Oswald opened their own grocery store, Ferndell, at the corner of Seaver and Barstow Streets. Ferndell was a high-quality canned goods brand that they carried. Sigurd was well-known in musical circles in town. His name was often mentioned in the paper connected to performances in many venues around the city.

Sigurd married Mildred Tait of La Crosse in 1922, but by 1930, she had become a bit disillusioned with Sigurd and their marriage. Perhaps one of the reasons for this was named Harriet. Sigurd and Harriet had been in a relationship for two years, and for most of that time, Harriet had no idea he was married. He had made love to her and convinced her to try alcohol with him. When she found out that he was married, she ended the relationship, but he did not stop pursuing her.

According to Harriet's coworkers at the Eau Claire Asylum, Sigurd would often sit outside the building, waiting for her to finish her shift. A few weeks earlier, he had told her that he was getting a divorce and that they could be together. He even took her to his home at 1527 Drummond. But by mid-December 1930, he had stopped calling.

Life got a bit complicated for Sigurd the week before Christmas in 1930. A few months earlier, Mildred had moved out with their son. A local judge was trying to reconcile the couple, and he talked Mildred into moving back in the week before Christmas.

After learning Sigurd was getting a divorce, Harriet was confused when she did not hear from him. On December 24, 1930, Harriet was downtown, keeping an eye on the Ferndell store. As she watched Sigurd working in the store, she phoned from a nearby phone booth and was told that he was not available and had not come into work that day. So, she sat quietly and waited for him to leave the store. Harriet had drunk a pint of moonshine earlier in the afternoon, trying to bolster her courage to confront Sigurd.

After Sigurd left the store, Harriet flagged a taxi and went to the block of Drummond where he lived. As she knocked on the door, demanding to see him, he sent his wife and son upstairs. He tried to reason with Harriet, telling her that he would come and see her later in the evening. She demanded he let her in right then, but he said no and locked the door. As he stood in front of the window, watching and waiting for her to leave, she pulled out a gun she had stolen that afternoon and shot it through the window several times.

During Harriet's trial, she said that she was not sure why she stole this gun. She bought another gun at the same time, but when the store owner's back was turned, she threw a second gun in her purse.

The three shots hit the window and grazed Sigurd's hand. He was not seriously hurt. Harriet took off, stole a car nearby and went to a roadside tavern Sigurd had taken her to from time to time. After neighbors called in complaints about gunshots and the missing car, the police finally tracked Harriet down at the tavern and arrested her with the gun in her possession. The officer said she had obviously been drinking.

Sigurd and Mildred moved across the country to California almost immediately. When the trial began a few months later, he was already settled in their new city and had to travel to Eau Claire for the court proceedings. It was briefly mentioned in the *Leader Telegram* a few months later that the Linds were unable to come to Sigurd's parents' fiftieth anniversary celebration because they were living in California.

Harriet was released on $4,000 bail a week after being arrested. At the trial, she explained the relationship she had with Sigurd and the fact that she had not known he was married until late in their affair. Her coworkers testified that she was of good character. She said she had been drinking that day and did not remember why she bought one gun or stole the other. Although she didn't seem to remember much about purchasing the gun, she admitted she recognized the clerk's face when she saw him in court. The clerk also said that when Harriet came to his store, she had obviously been drinking.

It didn't hurt Harriet's case that she appeared at the trial in a wheelchair with gashes on her face, a fractured wrist, a sprained ankle and several other minor injuries. Not long before the trial, she was in a car with her brother and sister-in-law when a drunk driver hit four cars, including theirs, putting Harriet in the hospital for a few weeks.

Judge Wickham explained to the jurors that they had three verdicts to consider: "guilty of assault with intent to murder as charged by the state, guilty of simple assault without the intent to murder, or not guilty." After giving further instructions, he ended by reminding the jury that it was "not the policy of the law to convict an innocent person, but on the other hand, neither is it the policy of the law to acquit a guilty one."

The jury acquitted a sobbing Harriet, obviously blaming Sigurd for his bad decision-making and for carrying on with a younger woman while lying about his marital status. However, the judge did decide that both the gun Harriet bought and the one she stole would go back to the store owner.

Grave marker for Harriet Butcher Jasper in Prairie View Cemetery, Chippewa Falls, Wisconsin. *Courtesy Diana Peterson.*

I wish I could report that Harriet and Mildred had a happy ending, but that was not the case. Sadly, within five years of the trial, both Harriet and Mildred were dead. Mildred Lind passed away in Los Angeles in 1935.

In 1934, Harriet married a Chippewa Falls man, Peter Jasper. Harriet died giving birth at the Deaconess Hospital in Minneapolis. Her newborn and her husband survived her, but I could find no record of her infant, so perhaps the baby did not live long. Harriet is buried at Prairie View Cemetery in Chippewa Falls. Her simple tombstone reads, "Harriet Jasper, Daughter, 1901–1935."

As for Sigurd Lind? He lived to be seventy-six and spent the rest of his life in sunny Anaheim, California.

A sad story with an even sadder ending.

Chapter 5

HOPEVALE MARTYRS

by Diana Peterson

T he horrors of World War II came to Eau Claire in a personal and
heartbreaking way in 1945.

The Reverend Erle Rounds and his wife, Louise, were members
of First Baptist Church in Eau Claire. The church was built in 1861 at 416
Niagara Street. First Baptist was an American Baptist church. The Southern
Baptists broke away from the General Baptist Church in 1845 because they
believed in slavery and the General Baptists did not. American Baptists tend
to be more liberal in their doctrine, liturgical in their worship and ecumenical
in their practice.

In 1899, the Baptist Missionary Union (BMU) began organizing an
overseas mission, and in 1901, the Evangelical Union of the Philippines
began. In 1924, the American Baptists took over the Iloilo Mission Hospital,
which had been started by the Presbyterians. The BMU also supported
Central Philippines University and Filamer Christian University. The
missionaries were primarily educators and healthcare workers.

In 1930, Erle and Louise Round were accepted as missionaries to the
Philippines, an American territorial possession. They traveled east to spend
a few days at the Kennedy School of Missions in Hartford, Connecticut, and
the American Baptist Foreign Mission Society in New York before returning
to Eau Claire for their commission service.

The Rounds spent several years in the Philippines before returning to Eau
Claire in the mid- to late '30s. After some time raising money and visiting
American churches, the couple was ready to return to their work in the

Philippines with their two sons, nine-year-old Donal and two-year-old Erle. Their trip back might have been an omen, because it was a difficult crossing. Their first ship, the *President Coolidge*, was shipwrecked; later, they boarded the *President Jackson*. Halfway to the Philippines, they ran into a typhoon, and everything movable had to be tied down with rope. Louise tried to write letters home, but the sea was so rough that her typewriter would not stay on the table. One of the crew mentioned that he had made sixty-seven crossings, and this was the worst.

When World War II began, the Round family, along with the other missionaries in the compound, made the decision to stay in the Philippines to continue their work. The names of the missionaries serving at the time were Jennie Adams; James and Charma Covell; Dorothy Dowell; Signe Erickson; Dr. Frederick Meyer and his wife, Ruth; Dr. Francis Rose and his wife, Gertrude; and the Round family. In December 1941, less than twelve hours after attacking Pearl Harbor, Japan attacked the Philippines. When the Japanese invaded the island, General Douglas MacArthur withdrew his troops to fight elsewhere, and the eleven American Baptist missionaries refused to surrender to the Japanese troops.

In April 1942, the group fled to the mountains of Barrio Katipunan and hid in a forest. Donal Rounds was living at an international school in Manila, and his parents felt he would be safer staying there. Dr. Rose suggested their new home be called Hopevale. They built several thatched houses and an outdoor chapel known as Cathedral in the Glen.

For twenty months, the missionaries were supported by local Filipinos who risked their own lives to bring them food, supplies and news from the outside world. Up to one hundred people often joined them in worship on Sundays. The missionaries served the American-supported Filipino guerrillas. Several American miners also lived in the area. It was not an easy place to live, even in the best of circumstances. They had to deal with mosquitoes, leeches, heavy rain and mud daily.

In 1943, an American soldier, Lieutenant Albert King, was captured and tortured until he disclosed the location of the missionaries. On December 19, 1943, Japanese troops arrived at Hopevale during a Sunday church service. Five miners remained with the missionaries: Mark and Fern Clardy; their two sons, Johnny and Terry; and a miner known as Mr. King.

Captain Watanabe and his troops arrested the missionaries and the miners. There was a disagreement about what to do with the prisoners. One of the officers was waiting for word from his superiors, citing prior instructions to jail Americans but not to kill them. Another Japanese fighting unit came

Replica of the Cathedral in the Glen at Hopevale, located at the Green Lake Conference Center, Green Lake, Wisconsin. *Courtesy Green Lake Conference Center.*

onto the scene. Their lead commander, who outranked the arresting officer, decided all the prisoners should be put to death.

The captured Americans were brought into a room one by one and beheaded by Captain Watanabe with his sword. Rather than behead the children, Watanabe killed them with a bayonet. After everyone had been murdered, the Japanese set the house on fire to destroy any evidence. Two weeks later, Pastor Dianala and Engracio Arora risked their lives to recover the remains in the charred ruins. They buried them under the floor of the pastor's church. Later, the remains were taken to Hopevale and buried beneath a large cross.

The U.S. War Department notified the relatives of the missionaries that they had died during the war, but it was not until 1945 that their families learned how they were killed. Donal Rounds was taken to a concentration camp in Manila and was freed by General MacArthur's troops when they returned to the Philippines. He was reunited with his Eau Claire relatives in early June 1945.

The group of murdered missionaries came to be known as the Hopevale Martyrs. This group has been honored in several places. A replica of the cross under which they were buried is located at Central Philippine University.

A two-act musical drama titled *Hopevale: Memories of Missions and Martyrs* was performed at Central Philippine University in 2005. Two books have been written about the tragedy: *No Greater Love: Triumph and Sacrifice of American Baptist Missionaries during WWII Philippines, and the Martyrdom in Hopevale* by Wilma Rugh Taylor, Elmo D. Familiaran and Ann Qualls (2007) and *The Edge of Terror* by Baptist minister Scott Walker (2009).

A church in Saginaw, Michigan, is named Hopevale Church in the missionaries' memory. There is also a replica of the Cathedral in the Glen at the Green Lake Conference Center (formerly the American Baptist Conference Center) in Green Lake, Wisconsin. Jennie Adams, the nurse with the group, was also a poet, and her poetry is displayed along the walk as visitors enter the cathedral in the woods.

While World War II was filled with tragic tales—and many Eau Claire residents were scarred by the poignant stories of their loved ones—this killing of sixteen innocent people who were just trying to love and help others is truly a horrific one.

PART II

NOTABLE WOMEN OF EAU CLAIRE

Chapter 6

BERENICE BRINGS HOME THE BACON

by Jodi Kiffmeyer

The caption for a photo in the Chippewa Valley Museum's archives reads, "Eau Claire's first businesswoman." Berenice Culver Ellison might have been the first woman in town to own a business outside her home. Certainly, women had engaged in "cottage" businesses—things like sewing clothing, making hats, giving music lessons—from their homes for decades before that. Still, Berenice is an interesting woman to know.

Berenice was probably one of those women who started a business because she had to learn to fend for herself. Her first husband, Samuel Ellison, was a Civil War veteran and successful businessman who started drinking heavily and lost his fortune. He periodically went "into the woods" to work and was good at it—when sober. Staying that way was easy in the lumber camps, where alcohol generally wasn't allowed; it was when Sam came to town that he ran into trouble. With a wife and children living in town, Sam was between the forest and a hard place.

In 1874, Berenice divorced Sam. A few months later, he headed to her house with a revolver, threatening to shoot her and himself. She escaped harm, but Sam died of suicide that day. At the time of her husband's death, Berenice had been in the music business for a few years already, working for Edward Allen, who sold pianos, organs and sewing machines on East Grand Avenue (then known as Kelsey Street). Berenice was known as his best saleslady. The 1890 city directory says she also ran a boardinghouse at 411 South Farwell, another common occupation for women.

The *Eau Claire Weekly Leader* announced Berenice was opening her own store in May 1891, after she made a trip to the East to purchase a stock of pianos and organs. She shared the space at 308 South Barstow Street with a fellow businesswoman, Mrs. Cordelia Cook, a milliner (hatmaker). They both moved to 304 South Barstow Street early in 1893. Mrs. Cook wasn't there for long, and by 1898, Harry Covert of Chicago was renting the other half of the store for his own millinery shop.

What kind of businesswoman was Berenice? She had some spice to her. She wasn't afraid to hold her own when she thought someone had taken advantage of her. Harry Covert discovered this in July

Berenice Culver Ellison, 1880. *Courtesy Chippewa Valley Museum.*

1898, when Berenice lost a ten-dollar bill in her store and accused him of stealing it. The *Eau Claire Leader* did a colorful job of painting the picture:

> *Mrs. Ellison and Mr. Covert said things to each other. Mrs. Ellison ordered her tenant to evacuate and insisted on an unconditional surrender. Like Uncle Sam she voluntarily and at her own expense had the enemy's implements of warfare—his Paris bonnets, ostrich plumes, old point lace, artificial flowers, etc.—piled in rich profusion on the sidewalk.*

Mr. Covert's letter to the editor the following day had an "Oh, yeah? Well, I was leaving anyway!" quality to it. The reader gets the distinct impression that Mrs. Ellison won that battle.

The following year, Berenice used the newspaper to air a complaint against the Rust Owen Lumber Co., which owned the building where she had her store. Early in August 1899, Rust Owen gave her a notice to vacate within thirty days so the Kepler & Co. dry goods store could expand their storefront on Kelsey Street. This time, possibly because of the difference in power dynamics, Berenice sounded a little passive aggressive when writing an advertisement in the *Leader* for her upcoming liquidation sale. According to her, the sudden move was a "surprise" and a "hardship," because she'd just returned from buying stock in the East, but she promised to vacate with a smile and move to an office across the street from the public library. She added that she'd been planning to leave the building by January 1 anyway, sounding a little bit like Harry Covert did when she bested him.

It's hard to say if Berenice followed through on her plans for an office near the library. The 1900 directory still lists her at 304 South Barstow, possibly because it was printed before the change took place. In 1902, she was selling pianos from her home at 917 South Farwell, and she continued to do so for several years.

In 1915, at age seventy-five, Berenice married Samuel Converse, a general contractor, though he lived only a few years after the wedding. When she herself died on a trip to Minneapolis in 1925, she left a considerable fortune, including real estate in Florida.

Chapter 7

A ROYAL HEAD ON HER SHOULDERS

by Jodi Kiffmeyer

Eva Converse was a woman of many accomplishments, the kind of lady the teenaged girls of Eau Claire would have dreamed of becoming. She was a singer and actress. She had a successful career as a model, which at the time meant sitting still for hours while an artist dabbed paint on a canvas. If we're to believe the local newspaper accounts, she started a three-year grand tour of Europe in 1901 at the age of sixteen. Those same papers were writing about Eva's doings in Eau Claire a few years before she admitted to being born, so maybe we take her age with a grain of salt. Nevertheless, there's no doubt Eva made a splash in the world wherever she happened to land. What she's most famous for, though, is her beheading.

It started on that tour of Europe. Her letters appeared in the *Eau Claire Leader* a few times throughout 1902, chatty missives in which she talks about crossing the English Channel, spending Christmas at Westminster Abbey, sailing down the Rhine in a friend's yacht and dining with "one of the great Princes of India" at a hotel in Paris. To the casual reader back in Eau Claire, she probably sounded pretentious, a trifle tiresome. Believe it or not, she left out the really impressive bits.

Those came a few years later, in May 1905, when the *Minneapolis Sunday Times* spilled a secret Eva had been keeping for a couple years. The article, titled "Royal Head Rests on Her Shoulders," reported an interview

Portrait of Eva Converse from January 5, 1911, on the cover of the *Youth's Companion*. *Public domain, courtesy HathiTrust.*

with Miss Converse about Edwin Abbey's painting of King Edward VII's coronation.

In Eva's own words: "When Edwin Abbey, the great American artist… was selected to paint the coronation picture of King Edward VII and Queen Alexandria, he was confronted with an obstacle. Although the queen is noted for her facial beauty, she lacks in symmetry of shoulders and that delicacy of outline in arms and shoulders to accord with the rest of her beauty."

With the brashness of an American citizen separated from the Queen of England by one whole ocean and half a continent, Eva continues, "If you notice most of the pictures of Queen Alexandra you can see that she is usually pictured with her arms tightly sheathed in gloves and heavy jewelry about her neck and over her shoulders. It is well known that the queen has a birthmark on her neck. In the coronation picture however it was necessary for the model to be free of all blemishes."

While pondering his dilemma, Abbey had the fortune to meet Eva Converse at a reception at the U.S. embassy in London. The former Eau Claire girl was already drawing attention from the cosmopolitan crowd. She was engaged to Efflatoum Bey, a painter and varsity rower for Cambridge University, rumored to be the son of a Russian nobleman and a French countess living in Egypt. A New York newspaper described Bey's infatuation with Eva, asking, "What could be prettier on canvas than the fiancee's shell-pink skin and her dusky black hair and her eyes that are sometimes gray? And those arms, so exquisitely modelled!" At the embassy, Abbey made small talk with Miss Converse before coming right out and declaring, "What beautiful hands you have." He invited Eva to visit his studio the following day.

Eva kept the appointment. When she arrived, the artist asked her to change into a gown that would show off her assets—with assistance from his wife, of course, for propriety's sake. When Eva complied, he studied her arms, shoulders and hands and declared, "I have never found the right person…till I saw you." He asked her to wear the queen's coronation robes and serve as a body double—just her body—in the official painting.

The painting pleased King Edward—at least, he liked it well enough to hang it at Buckingham Palace. Eva discovered she enjoyed modeling and embarked on a career that lasted for years and put her on the canvases of Dutch painter Lawrence Alma-Tadema and the cover of a popular American magazine, *Youth's Companion*. She was an actress in early silent films as well. The only drawback to her modeling career, according to Eva, was that she found it "tedious" sitting for students. "To be stared at and sketched by a crowd of embryo [artists] is one of the burdens of the work. After posing for a really great artist, a model, I'm afraid, is spoiled."

One can almost hear Queen Alexandra grumbling, "Off with her head!"

Chapter 8
ROSENKRANS (AND ABERCROMBIE)

by Jodi Kiffmeyer

Helen Rosenkrans was one of the most remarkable women in Eau Claire history. She was born in 1859 in Columbia, Wisconsin, the youngest child of the Reverend Cyrus and Helen S. Rosenkrans. Cyrus was a Congregational minister and a teacher. Despite a strong family connection to higher education—Reverend Rosenkrans helped to start the Columbia Collegiate Institute in 1855—evidence suggests Helen never made it past the eighth grade. But she did a lot with the education she had.

Helen appeared in the Eau Claire city directory for the first time in 1882, listed as a teacher at the North Side Branch School. In 1885, she began a photography career in partnership with Edward E. Fawcett of Fawcett & Co. She spent a few years as a photographer in Oregon between 1889 and 1895 before returning to Eau Claire to set up her own studio at 401 South Barstow. Ironically, although the museum owns more than forty photos taken by Helen, there's only one that includes her. In it, she sits at the far side of the table at a dinner party. Decades later, the daughter of the couple who hosted the party wrote "Mrs. Rosenkrans" on the reverse side of the print, although Helen never married.

Helen did have an extraordinarily close lifelong relationship with Eleanor "Ella" Abercrombie, the daughter of a well-to-do bookseller with a shop at 205 South Barstow Street. The Abercrombie family lived in the house that's still standing at 109 Marston Avenue. Helen moved into the home around 1896, after returning from Oregon, and remained there with Ella after her father died in 1899. The kind of arrangement they had was often called a

Men and women at a dinner party in 1900. Helen Rosenkrans is fourth from right. *Courtesy Chippewa Valley Museum.*

"Boston marriage," named for a pair of characters in Henry James's 1886 novel *The Bostonians.* In the book, Olive Chancellor and Verena Tarrant do what independent single women like them frequently did during that era—they formed a long-term partnership, living together and sharing expenses. For women of the time, sometimes this was a necessity, sometimes a preference. Some Boston marriages had a romantic component, and some didn't. Either way, it was considered a respectable way of life at the time, as long as the women involved were discreet about the nature of their relationship. We don't know many details about Helen and Ella's relationship, other than that they lived together for at least forty-five years.

From August 1908 to August 1909, Helen was editor of the women's section of the *Eau Claire Leader*, which appeared weekly on Sundays. During her tenure, she published articles about wealth management and politics, alongside the more traditional women's subjects like society news and meal planning. She wrote for others, too. Magazines in Chicago and San Francisco published her work, and she won a literal ton of gas coke fuel in a poetry contest sponsored by Eau Claire Gas Light Co. The first stanza sets the tone for the other three:

The high class bards in tuneful mood
To strains of love their lyres awoke,
But I shall sing of hotter stuff,
The praises of PURE GAS COKE

Helen began her most ambitious project in 1916, when she started her own monthly news magazine, aptly titled the *Rosenkrans Magazine* (later the *Chippewa Valley*). Again, she didn't stick exclusively, or even primarily, to traditional women's topics. Her focus was the "cutover" region, the stump-riddled and brush-clogged acres of land north of Eau Claire that were left behind after the lumber industry clear-cut the useful timber. Helen used her magazine to champion efforts to bring farmers to the cutover and the construction of good roads that would allow travel between towns and rural areas.

The *Chippewa Valley* continued until about 1922, when Helen and Ella began traveling frequently and for long periods of time to Colorado and California. They eventually left Eau Claire for good in 1926, moving to Carmel, California. They lived there for the rest of their lives. Ella died in 1939. Her obituary, written by Helen, begins, "Early Tuesday morning a beautiful life passed out of this earth leaving sad and lonely hearts behind." Helen lived with a niece after Ella was gone and died in Santa Clara, California, in 1942.

Chapter 9

ROSE KING: LOCAL ROYALTY

by Diana Peterson

Rose Koenig was born in Eau Claire in 1884, graduating from high school in 1902. Her father, Frederick, was a local gunsmith (her mother was Amanda). Rose grew up at 727 Second Avenue; her father owned a lot of the land in the area near the courthouse. She had five siblings: a brother (August) who was a jeweler and four sisters (Edith, Emily, Ernestine and Maxine), three of whom were dressmakers in their adult years.

Rose was involved in a lot of school and community events. She was a part of the senior class committee, and one of the activities they had planned was a trolley ride for seniors. Two trolley cars were decked out in white and yellow, the class colors.

The name Rose King was more than a stage name. Growing up, Rose and her siblings felt that "Koenig" was, more often than not, mispronounced, so they all changed their name to King for daily life. However, Rose's high school graduation program listed her as Koenig, and so does her gravestone. Her parents, who emigrated from Germany after the Civil War, felt strongly about keeping their original surname.

After graduation, Rose traveled with her ill sister Emily to Denver, Colorado. She had an interest in acting, but her only experience had been her senior class play, *A Perplexing Situation*. She asked to try out at one of the summer stock companies in Denver, and they accepted her. In the fall, she joined a barnstorming troupe visiting mining towns and smaller cities. Rose earned $1.50 a day, which paid for her meals and lodging. She was supposed

Rose King posing in the 1920s. *Courtesy Chippewa Valley Museum.*

to get another $15 a week, but that rarely happened. The company went broke in Walla Walla, Washington, so Rose took a steamer to San Francisco, where Emily was then living. She joined another stock company there, performing in *Shenandoah*, a Civil War melodrama.

Rose was summoned to New York about 1905 with three other actors from her group to appear in *Judge and Jury*. The play only lasted two weeks, but while in New York, Rose found an agent. For the next three decades, Rose was never out of work.

In 1907, James Corbett, nicknamed Gentleman Jim, chose Rose as his leading lady. Corbett's biography, *The Roar of the Crowd*, became *Gentleman Jim* on the big screen, starring Errol Flynn. James J. Corbett was known as the originator of modern boxing, relying on science in his training. In 1892, he became world heavyweight champion when he beat John L. Sullivan, who had thirty pounds on Corbett. Corbett kept the heavyweight championship for six years, losing to Bob Fitzsimmons in 1898.

Corbett also got involved with baseball. He played exhibition games on tour. His brother Joe pitched for the Orioles, and one of his best friends, John Montgomery Ward, was the Giants manager/player.

Corbett pursued a career in acting after graduation. When he became world champ, a play was written about him, and he performed that around the country. After retiring from the ring, he went back to acting.

In 1908 Corbett and King starred in a play, *The Burglar and the Lady*, about a gentleman burglar who is also a detective, which helps to shield his more shady pastime. They traveled the country performing and made a stop in Eau Claire at the opera house there. Tickets cost $.25 to $1, and the house was sold out.

The *Leader Telegram* determined that "Rose is a fine young lady who by hard work has worked her way up from the mast so to speak to the head of her profession. She is an eminently handsome lady of a pleasing personality and a stately figure. She will grace any position that may be assigned her."

By 1910, Rose was living in Newport, Rhode Island. She and Edward Lynch started the King-Lynch Players of Manchester, New Hampshire, in 1912.

Rose began her Broadway career in 1919. One of her favorite plays was *The American Idea*, a musical comedy written by George Cohan. She also appeared in *The Torch Bearers*. The play was about a housewife who becomes an actress when her husband is away on business.

During her career, she also starred in twelve films including *The Necklace* and *The Seventh Day*, both costarring Mary Pickford and directed by D.W. Griffith.

In *The Necklace*, Harriet Leroque Kendrick (King's role) is a charming young lady with big dreams who grew up in a family of clerks and is always craving luxury. Harriet's husband loves her and tries to indulge her. When they are invited to a reception for a foreign prince, he pawns his watch to buy her a beautiful gown. Never satisfied, she complains she has no jewelry worthy of the gown. She borrows a necklace from a friend, but it's stolen at the party. Not wanting to admit to the loss, the couple buys a new one, needing to take out loans and work second jobs to pay it off—which takes decades. When it is paid in full, Harriet's guilt prods her to tell the truth about the necklace to her friend, who informs her the original necklace was a fake. She gives Louise the expensive necklace back, but by then, Louise is worn out, and she dies shortly after.

In *The Seventh Day*, a neglectful woman wants custody of her children after a divorce. The judge rules that he will give her custody only if she can demonstrate her children's love for her within a week. In 1909, the *Eau Claire Leader* reviewed *The Seventh Day*, which was playing in Eau Claire. It described Rose as "a lady of great personal charms, her body being as graceful as the body of a panther."

Rose spent much of her theatrical career in partnership with B.M. York. Their most famous skit was "The Old Family Tintype." The couple had an international following and toured both the United States and England.

Rose returned to Eau Claire after retiring from show business in 1942, residing at a home at 731 Second Avenue with her sister. A fire in the attic later destroyed most of her professional souvenirs. After returning to Eau Claire, Rose rented out two apartments and a cottage. In a 1947 *Leader Telegram* photograph, she can be seen picketing on Graham Avenue. She and several other landlords were angry about the restrictions the Office of Price Administration was placing on rentals. Rose's sign said, "OPA is not the American way."

In 1958, Rose was diagnosed with tuberculosis, and she moved to the Mount Washington Sanitarium for eight months.

None of Rose's siblings married, and she was the last surviving member of her family. She passed away in 1967 and is buried in Lake View Cemetery.

Chapter 10

MEET AGNES BARLAND MCDANIEL

by Diana Peterson

I'd like to introduce you to Agnes Barland McDaniel. To get to know Agnes, it helps to start with her grandparents, Herman and Augusta Schlegelmilch, and the values they passed on to their family.

Herman was born in Suhl, Germany, in 1830, a city known for gun manufacturing. He apprenticed in his uncle's rifle factory and eventually made his way to the United States. After spending some time in New York and Pennsylvania, he landed in Beaver Dam, Wisconsin, in 1855, where he opened a gun shop.

Augusta Emilie Krueger was born in 1832 in Domitz, Germany, into a wealthy family. She also found herself embarking on a journey to the United States in 1853, settling in Milwaukee, where she supported herself cleaning houses and sewing. She then moved to Beaver Dam to become a housekeeper for her brother Ferdinand.

It was inevitable that Herman and Augusta would meet in Beaver Dam. They fell in love and married in 1858. In 1859, their first child, daughter Dora, was born. A few years later, Herman and Augusta moved to Eau Claire. They bought a building at 312 Eau Claire Street for their gun shop, living on the second floor. In 1866, Herman began building a new brick store at 217 South Barstow; while he still crafted guns, this shop was a general hardware store. A lot of sources refer to this building as the first brick business in Eau Claire. By 1871, Herman and Augusta had welcomed five more children: Louisa, born in 1862; Carl, born in 1864, who died at two months; Emilie, born in 1865; Herman F., born in 1867; Ferdinand, born in 1871, who did not survive; and Eda, born in 1873.

In 1871, Herman decided his larger family needed a larger house, and they moved to the corner of Jones and Farwell, a tree-lined neighborhood. (Jones later became Lake Street.)

Dora married local farmer John Barland and raised her large family nearby. Herman F. married Kate Chadwick. They had two daughters, who lived in Eau Claire until Herman passed away in 1924; they then moved to California with their mother, keeping close ties with their Eau Claire relatives. Louisa, Emily and Eda remained in the house until they passed away. When Herman died, he made sure all his children were well provided for. In addition to the money and businesses they were gifted, he left the house to his daughters.

By 1927, Louise was alone in the house. She had seen the death of two of her brothers in infancy, Eda at age nineteen from typhoid, her father in 1903, her mother in 1920, her brother in 1924 and her sister Emilie in 1926. Dora was the only other sibling still alive. Louise kept busy maintaining the house, visiting with friends, attending social events and traveling with Dora's family.

Louise was close to all her nieces and nephews and their children. They often visited her and, at times, lived at the house temporarily. Before Louise passed away in 1949, she made the decision to leave the house to Dora's daughter Agnes Louise Barland McDaniel.

Agnes had a very interesting life. The years 1890 to 1917 were known as the Progressive Era, when women had more educational options available, more careers to choose from and a variety of social clubs for their personal growth. Born in 1891, Agnes benefited from these changes.

After graduation, Agnes attended Oberlin College, a progressive school that began admitting women in 1835. She received her bachelor of arts degree in 1914 and her master of arts from Columbia Teachers College in 1917. She then attended Johns Hopkins School of Nursing, where she graduated second highest in her class.

From 1921 until 1927, Agnes lived in Siam (now Thailand) as a missionary. She helped establish the first school of nursing in northern Siam at McCormick Hospital, where she later became the supervisor of nursing.

When Agnes's father became ill in 1928, she returned to Eau Claire. She began corresponding with Dr. Edwin McDaniel, whom she met in Siam, where he ran a mission hospital and a leper sanitorium in Nakon Sritamarat. His wife had recently passed away. Agnes and Edwin became closer through their correspondence, and they were married in Penang, Siam, in 1932.

Agnes was a great storyteller. She liked to tell one anecdote about giving a dinner party in Siam. During the party, she called a servant over and asked him to put a bowl of milk on the floor by the door. When he did so, a boa constrictor slithered out from under the table and over to the milk, where they were able to kill it. Asked how she knew there was a boa under the table, Agnes admitted that she had felt it against her legs.

Agnes brought back a lot of souvenirs from her time in Thailand, including a python skin; the skull of a man-eating tiger; elephant figurines, including one that was a princess's paintbox; and a collection of books that were four thousand years old.

Agnes Barland in 1914 at her Oberlin graduation. *Courtesy Chippewa Valley Museum.*

While Agnes and her husband were in Siam, they met fellow missionary Margaret Landon, who ran a mission school in Trang. In 1956, Agnes talked with a *Leader Telegram* reporter about one of Margaret's visits with the couple at their home. By Agnes's account, she and Edwin drove "20 miles over rickety roads into the jungle to meet [Margaret] when she got off the tiny train."

Later, after their lunch, Margaret said, "How good it is to just rest. I'm going to my room to just sleep and read this afternoon." According to Agnes, Edwin told Margaret, "'I think I have the very books you would enjoy.' He gave her two books that he always kept hidden behind the other books. The Royal family had banned them." They were *An English Governess at the Siamese Court* and *Romance of the Harem*, published in 1870 and 1873. The stories were by Anna Leonowens, and they were based on her life in the 1860s working at the palace of King Mongkut as a governess for his children.

Margaret thought the information was fascinating but the writing was not, so she decided to rewrite the stories into one book. She titled it *Anna and the King of Siam*, which became the movie *The King and I* with Yul Brynner and Deborah Kerr. We have Agnes and Edwin to thank for that.

Agnes also shared a letter with a *Leader Telegram* reporter that she had in her collection. It was written by King Mongkut to the English governor of Hong Kong in 1855. She said Edwin had found it between pages of a book he purchased at a used bookstore in London.

Agnes Barland riding an elephant in Chaing Mai, Siam, 1923. *Courtesy Chippewa Valley Museum.*

In 1935, Edwin became ill and had a stroke. He traveled to the Mayo Clinic in Rochester after spending some time with Agnes's family in California. On his return to Siam, his health issues continued, and he was forced to retire and return to the United States in 1937, where he lived for only a short time.

After Edwin's death, Agnes taught in Puerto Rico and was a house mother at Wheaton College in Illinois for a few years. When her brother became ill, she returned to Eau Claire to help run the Barland Agency from 1942 to 1946. She lived with Louise at the family home before inheriting it on Louise's death in 1949. From 1946 until 1970, she traveled with family, attended local church meetings and spent quality time with her friends.

In 1978, Agnes gifted her home to the Chippewa Valley Museum and moved into the Syverson Home, where she passed away in 1982.

Like her grandparents, Agnes prioritized helping others, understood the importance of a good education and appreciated traveling, the lessons it taught her and the importance of experiencing life to the fullest. Her family equipped her to experience an interesting, adventurous and charitable life.

Chapter 11

ELVA CLASS: A POLITICIAN IN HER SPARE TIME

by Jodi Kiffmeyer

The first woman to run for city council in Eau Claire didn't succeed. The *Eau Claire Leader* announced her candidacy on February 23, 1930, with a headline reading, "Mrs. Elva Class First Woman to Seek Councilman Post." She had "assented to the insistent urgings of many of her women friends to get into the race." It was a crowded field—Elva was the fourteenth of a record number of people announcing their candidacies, and the newspaper speculated that one or two more would enter the ring by the deadline for primary candidates a few days later.

Born in Waukesha County, Wisconsin, in July 1877, Elva Nichols earned a bachelor of science degree from Milwaukee State Teachers College. In 1900, she married William Class, a bacteriologist working at the University of Chicago. William lived for only a short time after the marriage. When he died, Elva took over his research. The death of her sister-in-law in 1912 brought Elva to Eau Claire to care for her brother and two nieces, ages five and two.

Elva threw herself wholeheartedly into her new community. She became a leader in the PTA, the first commissioner for the Girl Scouts in the city, president of the Woman's Club and an active member of the Red Cross during the 1918 flu pandemic. In 1927, the *Eau Claire Leader* reported on a hospital visitation program she was supervising at the public library. Not only did she do most of the visits herself, but she also donated a collection of books to the program. Judging by a statement made in her obituary, people flocked to her home, which "was frequently a gathering place for young

Eau Claire City Council, 1955. *Courtesy Chippewa Valley Museum.*

people, individuals and discussion groups, and persons of prominence whose work brought them to Eau Claire."

By 1930, the nieces were grown, and Elva was probably looking for a challenge. Becoming the first woman on the city council was a good one. She wasn't a big spender. Two days before the primary, the *Leader* reported the expenditures of the candidates up to that point. The lone female in the field had spent $1.75, compared to the $93.54 put up by the most expensive campaign and still three times less than the next lowest budget, $6.30. She spent another $2.40 on an advertising insert placed in both the *Eau Claire Leader* and the *Eau Claire Telegram* before the election. She also appeared on the radio station WTAQ to talk about her philosophy of city government.

At the end of what was considered a quiet race, Elva ended up placing sixth, a "strong showing" according to many in the city. Indeed, she was in the top 50 percent of what ended up being a field of fifteen. Whatever disappointment she might have felt over the election didn't slow her down much. She made the news a couple weeks later as a featured speaker at a Women's Missionary Society tea. Her topic: "Glimpses of Japanese

Culture," based on a recent visit to Japan and the Hawaiian Islands. Elva's globetrotting ways also brought her to Russia, China, Samoa, Brazil and France. It seems running for city council was something she tried her hand at in between her other activities.

So who was the first woman on the city council in Eau Claire? Her name was Bessie Lee, and she was a housewife who had lived in the city for thirty years. The announcement of her candidacy in January 1955 was published in the newspaper with little fanfare, although they spelled her name "Betzy" and had to print a correction a few days later. Bessie served on the council for eight years. When she hung up her hat in 1963, her fellow council members gave her a commemorative gavel as a tribute to her work for the city.

Chapter 12

Jane Culver: She Stood Her Ground

by Diana Peterson

As Eau Claire residents, we have become accustomed to having a lot of famous authors in our midst: Nickolas Butler, Michael Perry, John Hildebrand, B.J. Hollars—and I could go on and on. However, that was not always the case. In 1934, a book was released in New York that caused quite a stir in the Eau Claire community.

So Stood I by Jane Culver was published by Houghton Mifflin in 1934. Culver, who was known as Mary Jane in Eau Claire circles, spent the first eighteen years of her life in the city. Her parents were both born in Eau Claire, and they married there in 1905. Jane's father, Joseph, was a real estate professional. Her mother was the former Mary McDonough. Jane grew up in two houses in Eau Claire: 312 Jefferson and 600 Oak Place. Mary Jane had other relatives still living in Eau Claire as well, namely the Wickams and the Welches. Her parents left Eau Claire for Florida and then moved to Akron, Ohio. Jane attended Columbia University. She lived in New York City but spent summers with her parents in Akron.

It took Mary Jane four years to write *So Stood I*. She said that many Eau Claire residents might recognize themselves in the book, but I never could find any accounts of people who did so. This was her first novel, and she wrote it using the stream-of-consciousness method made famous by James Joyce. The title of the book was taken from one of Emily Brontë's poems. An article in the *Leader Telegram* from 1934 describes a literary tea that was hosted for Culver by Houghton Mifflin to publicize her book.

A *New York Times* review said,

> [So Stood I] *introduces a writer of amazing maturity and imaginative understanding. It is a psychological novel, the experiences in the growth of a soul, from childhood, characterized by poetic imagination, keen emotional values and a cloak of fear—through adolescence, colored by the changed fortunes of the family. The heroine, having a religious conflict with her father, and realizing that her mother had a flawed, frivolous temperament, turns to her brother for love and understanding.*

It sounded so dramatic that I was surprised to read an article from the *New York Herald Tribune* by Margaret Cheney Dawson from 1934, who said the "virtues of her writing are abundant and tangible. It has a great personality, a flair for the newly bright, eye-opening phrase and frequent passages of delightful humor."

The book was available for sale in the Eau Claire Bookstore, where it sold very well. Another book that became available at the bookstore was a mystery by Thomas Polsky published in 1939.

Polsky was born in Akron in 1908. He was expected to take over as chairman of the Polsky's Department Store that his grandfather founded. Tom, who resisted going into business, went to Harvard, majoring in English. The Great Depression put an end to his business career, which he was happy about, having no interest in business. The department store continued until 1978 but in a more limited capacity, struggling with costs and the suburban malls and shopping centers that began popping up in the 1950s and '60s.

After graduating from Harvard, Thomas spent some time in Europe. On returning to the United States, he was offered a job as editor at the *Akron Times Press*. From 1930 to '34, he worked in several of the newspaper's departments. During his time there, a young woman approached him and asked if she could write some reviews for the paper. He liked her reviews, and he liked her—and they married in 1936. That woman was Mary Jane Culver.

Mary Jane took a sabbatical from writing to raise their two daughters. The couple searched for inspiring places to live in the United States and landed in Weaverville, North Carolina, near Asheville. After spending some time in the hospital in 1937, Thomas decided to try his hand at writing mysteries and never looked back.

The couple had a modern house with a terrace overlooking Mount Pisgah. They loved gardening, music and art. Thomas played both piano and cello. The couple opened up their home twice a year to host art exhibits. They contributed much of their time and income to local causes and enjoyed their life in Weaverville. Thomas passed away in 1976, while Mary Jane lived until 1991.

Mary Jane Culver's book is part of the LE Phillips Memorial Library Special Collections, and Thomas Polsky's books can be found on Amazon and other out-of-print vendors.

Mary Jane Culver's life sounds like it would make a fun plot for a novel. Maybe some young writer in Eau Claire will take up the challenge of capturing her story.

Chapter 13
CAN I GIVE YOU A LITTLE ADVICE?

by Diana Peterson

Eau Claire has had several famous residents. Two sisters lived here for a little over a decade but only became well-known after they moved away.

In 1918, identical twins were born seventeen minutes apart to Abraham and Rebecca Friedman in Sioux City, Iowa. The Friedmans owned a chain of theaters in their town. They had two older daughters, Dorothy and Helen. The couple named the twins Pauline Esther and Esther Pauline. Their father ran a movie house that featured vaudeville performers, and the sisters grew up playing violin and singing Andrews Sisters duets in Yiddish.

The girls graduated from Sioux City Central High School in 1936, and both wrote for their school newspaper. They continued writing when they attended Morningside College and cowrote a gossip column called the Campus Rat "with one byline, which was PEEP (for Pauline Esther/Esther Pauline)."

Pauline described their relationship: "Being a twin is a blessing that only a twin can know. It means never being lonely, having someone to share with—secrets as well as worldly goods."

The two seemed to do everything together, and in 1939, both girls dropped out of Morningside College two days before their twenty-first birthday to get married in a double ceremony. The wedding included three rabbis, a bridal party of twenty-two and seven hundred guests. The girls wore identical dresses, veils and hairstyles. Esther married Jules Lederer, and Pauline married Morton Phillips. Their husbands were drafted into the same World War II unit. After the war, both couples moved to Eau Claire,

Wisconsin. Morton was part of the Phillips family, who owned the National Presto Cooker Corporation. The two families lived in Eau Claire from 1944 to 1955. Morton was executive vice president of Martin Motors for Presto for a few years before becoming VP of National Presto. Jules started working at Johnson Printing in 1949 and then was hired at Presto in the early '50s.

Interviewed by Andrew Dowd for the *Leader Telegram* in 2013, Art Roach, a local resident, recalled that the sisters watched the Eau Claire Bears baseball games from their box seats. He said, "They were good fans. They were excellent baseball fans."

By 1956, they both had settled in different cities, Esther in Chicago and Pauline in San Francisco. They were offered jobs in the same field, and it caused a rift that first developed between the sisters while they lived in Eau Claire to deepen. They spent years not getting along, but luckily, they eventually reconciled.

So, who were these two women? You might know Esther better as Ann Landers from her column Ask Ann Landers. Pauline is widely known as Dear Abby.

So how did tension develop between the twins in Eau Claire? The Phillips family lived at 1603 Rust Street, while the Lederers lived at 1617 Valmont Avenue. The Lederers' home on Valmont was a modest one in the East Side Hill neighborhood; Esther referred to it as the Peanut Palace. The Phillipses earned significantly more money, and they were able to afford a house in the historic Third Ward. Esther's home was a bit newer, built in 1941, but it was a two-bedroom, one-bathroom, 676-square-foot home. The Phillips family settled into a 1936 home with three bedrooms, four bathrooms and more than 2,500 square feet.

Both sisters were hardworking socialites during their time in Eau Claire. Their list of activities and committees makes Donna Reed look a bit slothful. A partial list of what the two were involved in includes Community Chest, Gray Ladies, PTA, March of Dimes, Eau Claire County Association for the Disabled, Easter Seals, Salvation Army, B'nai Brith and YMCA, as well as a series of meetings with the governor about funding for an Alcoholic Treatment Center at St. Joseph's Hospital in Chippewa Falls. In addition to all that, Esther was very active in Democratic politics after a public tirade against Senator Joseph McCarthy.

The sisters threw elaborate costume parties, and they loved being the center of attention. One of their friends, Percy Atkinson, recalled that one day, right before a town parade began, the sisters just pulled in ahead of the band in a Cadillac convertible and led the troops, waving to the crowd.

"The Peanut Palace," the home of Esther/Ann Landers at 1617 Valmont Street in Eau Claire. *Courtesy Diana Peterson.*

The home of Pauline/Dear Abby at 1603 Rust Street in Eau Claire. *Courtesy Diana Peterson.*

While living in Eau Claire, Esther/Ann made the decision to acquire a new pert nose through surgery, which gave the sisters a distinguishable difference in appearance.

In 1949, Pauline/Abby traveled to Washington, D.C., with her daughter Jeanne, and she wrote a little article about the trip for the newspaper. She said Jeanne thought one of the passengers looked lonely. Jeanne struck up a conversation with him and ended up sitting by him most of the flight. It was Vice President Alben Barkley. He invited them to come to the White House, and seven-year-old Jeanne's response was that "they would love to, they ate there all the time"—referring to Austin's White House, a favorite Eau Claire restaurant.

In September 1952, the *Leader Telegram* featured an article about the Phillips family receiving an unusual delivery. Opening the crate, they found two cinnamon-ringtail monkeys from the jungles of Brazil. A Brazilian industrialist had spent some time with the family when he came to Eau Claire for two months to study production at Presto. After returning to Brazil, he sent the family their new pets. Morty had a large cage built next to the garage for the monkeys with a trapeze and insulated sleeping quarters. David was an extrovert, and Bathesheba was not. David was also more mischievous. One day he ate part of the clothesline, and another day he took a few tiles from the garage roof. Pauline/Abby's son Edward was not a fan, and he stated, "Monkeys should live with monkeys and people should live with people."

While living in Eau Claire in 1951, Pauline/Abby was given an opportunity to appear in a film, *At War with the Army*, which was shown at the State Theater. She played a minor part in a scene set in a nightclub; unfortunately, her two lines were cut from the final film. This was a Dean Martin and Jerry Lewis picture, starring Polly Bergen, about a song-and-dance team who were friends at one time. They reconnect in the military, but they have different ranks and lifestyles. They try to renew their friendship amid the differences in their social and economic statuses.

I can only wonder if the twins identified with the above plot a little more than they wanted to admit. When the sisters came to Eau Claire, they had everything in common. By the time they were ready to leave, there were a few holes in the relationship. Esther/Ann had changed her look, which was maybe more symbolic than she realized. With Esther living in the Peanut Palace, while her sister's home was four times that size, it must have been hard to constantly confront the economic and social differences between the two families.

After the families left Eau Claire in 1955, the Lederers headed for Chicago. Esther/Ann joined the *Chicago Sun-Times* and, three years later, took over an advice column penned by Ruth Crowley, who wrote as Ann Landers until she passed away in 1958. Esther/Ann beat out twenty-eight other applicants and was paid eighty-seven dollars a week. As Ann Landers, she received about two thousand letters a day. She had eight secretaries and two mail clerks to help deal with the deluge. If she did not have the knowledge she needed to answer a letter, she consulted a professional, adding her own wit and wisdom to the response. Her column was carried in thirty newspapers. After Crowley died, letters piled up for her at the *Sun-Times*, and the editor told Esther/Ann that her sister could help her get caught up on the backlog. However, after a short time, the *Sun-Times* decided two was one too many.

Once Pauline/Abby settled in San Francisco, she began writing an advice column for the *San Francisco Chronicle* as Dear Abby. She chose the name Abigail Van Buren to combine Abigail from the Bible and President Martin Van Buren. Like her sister, she consulted professionals when she needed to. If there was an urgent problem, she responded by letter immediately. Eventually, the Dear Abby column was syndicated in one thousand newspapers across the country, and it eclipsed her sister's advice column in popularity.

While the women both had liberal tendencies and senses of humor, Pauline/Abby became pro-choice before abortion was legal and defended the LGBT community before Esther/Ann did.

Even in the best of circumstances, it would have been hard to have competing columns. Now, in addition to their relationship as twins, they were seen as rivals. It didn't help to have the entire world sharing its own opinions. In 1958, a *Life* magazine article was headlined "Twin Lovelorn Advisors Torn Asunder by Success." The article described their relationship as "the most feverish female feud since Elizabeth sent Mary Queen of Scots to the chopping block."

Jeanne said after her mother, Pauline, was hired for her Dear Abby column, Esther/Ann did not talk to her for a decade. Jeanne said, "I have only seen my mother cry a few times in my whole life, and that was one." The sisters did reconcile later in life, but their relationship was never the same.

Both columns were written before 24-7 talk shows and the need for never-ending news and celebrity stories, so the questions and responses revealed a rare glimpse into the lives of average Americans, especially in the areas of sex and marriage. Almost everyone read the columns and talked about them over the water cooler.

Examples of Dear Abby's wit can be seen in many of her responses. When one woman mentioned that two men had bought a house together in her San Francisco neighborhood and were entertaining "a very suspicious mixture of people," she wondered, "How can we improve the neighborhood?" Abby's response was "You could move."

Another letter asked, "Dear Abby: I've been going with this girl for a year. How can I get her to say yes? Don." Abby's answer was "Dear Don: What's the question?"

Esther (Ann Landers) passed away in June 2002 in Chicago, and Pauline (Dear Abby) died in 2013 in Minneapolis.

In 1972, Pauline/Abby wrote a love letter to the city of Eau Claire. She mentioned a couple of her favorite things: costume parties at the Hotel Eau Claire and dinners at Austin's White House.

From my research, it sounds like the twins loved Eau Claire and Eau Claire loved them. I just wish they had left our city as close to each other as they were when they arrived.

PART III

MEN ABOUT TOWN

Chapter 14

THE NORWEGIAN REVOLUTIONARY

by Jodi Kiffmeyer

O nce upon a time in Eau Claire, there lived an old man who was nearly blind. He lodged with his son, a prominent doctor, in a simple room on the top floor of a house at 324 Water Street. He wore a floppy hat as he puttered around town on his frequent walks, his son's two bloodhounds in tow. Children were drawn to him and often trailed behind him, too. When he died, his family held a short secular service next to an unmarked grave in Lakeview Cemetery. Only a few friends were present. This simple life belied one of the most important labor and social reformers in Norwegian history.

Marcus Thrane was born in Christiania (now Oslo), Norway, in 1817. His father was arrested for corruption shortly after his birth, and Marcus was orphaned by age fifteen. At age twenty, he traveled through France, Germany and Switzerland, eventually settling in Paris for several months before returning to Norway at the end of the year. He studied theology for about a year, then moved to Lillehammer in 1841 to run a private school with his wife, Josephine Buch. She threw herself into Marcus's work alongside him.

Marcus was famous in Norway before coming to the United States. Most of his countrymen would have called him infamous. His ideas were considered radical at the time, though these days, many of them are seen as mundane. What did Marcus ask for? Things like universal voting rights (for men), intellectual freedom, education and political equality.

Marcus Thrane with dogs Figaro and Zampa, 1889. *Courtesy Chippewa Valley Museum.*

Europe was full of such ideas in the mid-nineteenth century. In February 1848, a political revolution began in France and swept across the continent. Marcus later wrote about how the news of the unrest affected him: "Then one day [the newspaper] came out with an account of the February revolution of 1848—of how the Fourth Class—the laboring class—suddenly demanded a voice and part in the government and refused to continue with the rule of the upper classes. Herewith came light to my gropings! I believed that my dreams might perhaps be realized."

Later that year, Marcus became the editor of a newspaper in Drammen, where he lived. Here he experienced the first resistance to his new mission. Unsurprisingly, people with excessive influence felt threatened by talk of rights and equality. His opinions turned off readers and alarmed his publishers. Subscriptions dropped, offering an easy excuse for Marcus's firing in December. The setback gave him the opportunity to pursue a project he'd already been considering. He started a newspaper of his own, the *Arbeiderforeningernes Blad* (*Labor Associations' Newspaper*), and published the first issue on May 5, 1849.

During these years, Marcus was also working to organize labor in Norway. He founded the Drammen Labor Union in late 1848; by 1849, the so-called Thranite Movement had spread across the country. The national coalition petitioned the ruling King Oscar II of Sweden and the Norwegian parliament for equality in education and suffrage, among other demands. With over thirteen thousand signatures, the petition had broad support from laborers, tenant farmers and others from the lower classes. However, the government rejected it, and Marcus was thrown into prison, along with more than one hundred of his associates.

In total, Marcus Thrane spent seven years of his life as a prisoner—four years in the Christiania city jail and a further three years in prison. While he was gone, his family made great sacrifices to support him. Marcus's favorite son, Arthur, seven years old in 1851, chose to live with him in the Christiania jail. During those years, Marcus held daily classes for his son, teaching him math, English, German, French and Latin. Josephine Thrane edited her husband's newspaper during those years and educated all the children after Marcus was transferred from jail to prison. She contracted tuberculosis during that time, later dying of the disease.

After his release in 1858, Marcus discovered the Thranite Movement had essentially vanished. Rather than starting over, he decided to study photography in Germany and became one of Norway's first photographers. He lived in various cities in Norway until his wife's death in 1862. A year later, Marcus moved to New York City to practice his craft. He migrated to Chicago in 1866, joined by Arthur, who had come to the United States the previous year. While in Chicago, Marcus founded two newspapers and edited a third. He started the first Norwegian theater in that city and wrote several plays. Thrane met prominent members of the labor movement, including August Spies, one of the leaders of Chicago's Haymarket Riot. Later, Marcus would testify at Spies's trial.

Meanwhile, young Arthur Thrane was studying medicine in Chicago at Rush Medical School. He moved to Eau Claire in 1875 to set up a practice, and his father joined him a few years later. Marcus returned to Norway only once during his living years. In 1883, Norwegian American reportedly asked him to travel to the mother country to advocate for Norway to become a republic. He was disappointed by the reception he received there and never returned.

Marcus died in Eau Claire in 1890. Opinions about him around town can best be summed up by the words of an obituary printed in Eau Claire's Norwegian-language newspaper, the *Reform*:

> *We are not able to evaluate his worth. Many of the ideas which so violently shook the earth there at home during the "Thranite movement" bear fresh sprouts, and the Norwegian working man is far on the way to independence and equality. His* [atheism] *and his inconsiderate and often indecent writings against individuals of other convictions, alienated many persons from him. It is said of him that he loved children and flowers. There was, after all, a heart also in Marcus Thrane's breast, despite all his bitterness and his frequently so stormy countenance.*

It wasn't until the mid-1900s that Norway began to appreciate Marcus Thrane's contributions to its history. In 1949, the country received permission from Thrane's surviving grandsons to exhume his body. It crossed the Atlantic and was reburied on May Day, Europe's Labor Day, at the Norwegian government's expense. His final resting place is an Oslo cemetery, in an area reserved for national heroes. The *News of Norway*, the official newspaper of the Norwegian embassy in Washington, D.C., concluded his obituary by saying, "Thrane's demands in the name of the Norwegian working people… today form the basis for one of the most advanced social programs to be found anywhere."

Chapter 15

HENRY HUDSON: NOT ASHAMED

by Jodi Kiffmeyer

Born in Mississippi around 1862, Henry Hudson likely spent his first few years of life in slavery. He came to Eau Claire around 1900, becoming one of only a handful of Black residents—or, as the *Eau Claire Leader* put it in its first mention of him in 1904, "an Ethiopian, unmixed blood." The article went on to describe him as "a very industrious man [who] deals in junk." Over the next sixteen years, Hudson made a name for himself in Eau Claire. In fact, we probably know more about him than any other Black man from the city's history.

Henry did indeed deal in junk, though today we'd probably consider it a recycling business combined with a thrift store. From his property on River Street (now Graham Avenue), he collected and resold shoes, hats, lace curtains, books, tires, rags, brass and any number of other materials that had outlasted their value for their original owners. It's easy to visit the former site of his business—just look for the steamboat landing marker along the Chippewa River, near the intersection of Graham and Gray Streets.

That location caused Henry some trouble. It was right across the street from the Federal Building, constructed in 1908 after several years of controversy over the proposed location. Henry's timing was poor when he petitioned the city council in 1907 for a permit to construct a frame building on his property. They denied him, claiming there were too many wooden buildings inside the city's fire limits. They didn't bother to conceal their true motivation: later in the meeting, when Alderman Lockwood proposed a resolution to "condemn, purchase or procure" Henry's property

Former site of Henry Hudson's business, 2024. *Courtesy Jodi Kiffmeyer.*

to "beautify" the government building, the motion carried on a vote of 14 to 5. Meanwhile, to explain why the council approved a nearly identical construction permit for the E.M. Fish Co., the *Eau Claire Leader* declared they drew a "color line."

The most devastating trouble came in 1920. On April 6, Henry and John Sather, a local detective, had an altercation on the steps of the Federal Building. After a brief scuffle, Sather fired a gun through his overcoat, hitting Henry twice in the abdomen and perforating his intestines. Henry died the following day. Sather was arrested and brought to trial.

Sather's defense largely consisted of raising questions about Henry's character. The prosecution must have known that many people in Eau Claire had better opinions of the dead man than Sather and his lawyers when he called on members of the public to come forward to defend Henry. In fact, a few days after Henry's death, the *Leader* published an eloquent eulogy by an anonymous writer:

> *Henry Hudson was a man of his word. His signature on a note meant security. His thrift and industry and honesty gave nobility even to the gathering of junk. He met his obligations when due. He need never to*

cross the street at the approach of a creditor in business transactions, he was honorable, and in his personal relations to his fellowmen he was honorable. He did not plan nor scheme to undermine or betray those with whom he associated.

Henry Hudson has now passed into the Great Beyond, but he leaves a memory in charitable minds of a man with head up, a contagious smile, and showing courage in the face of difficulties, very remarkable. By his own efforts and against great odds he had established a prosperous business, had gained the respect of those with whom he dealt, and had written himself on the books as a patriotic citizen. He acknowledged his duty to our common country and contributed to his ability to the aid of the government during the war. He did it unboastingly and from a sense of duty.

Is it a little thing to leave a memorial of backyards and alley-ways cleaner because he lived, and out of the gatherings to construct an estate and business of the proportions left by Mr. Hudson?

The writer knew what he was talking about. When all was accounted for, Hudson's estate was worth $14,243.82 (about $217,000 in 2023). Sadly, no one had the guts to defend his character at the trial, and Sather was acquitted on grounds of self-defense.

But let's give Henry the last word. In 1908, an unnamed trickster placed his name on the ballot for Eau Claire mayor, implying that the idea of a Black man in city government was laughable. Henry wrote a letter to the newspaper in response, clarifying he had no interest in the mayorship and adding that "he wasn't a monkey and not a tool." He ended with his proud signature, in the unstandardized spelling common at the time: "HENRY HUDSON is a man Not ashame of his callor."

Chapter 16
THE EAU CLAIRE PHOTOBOMBER

by Jodi Kiffmeyer

When you spend time looking at photos of the logging camps of the Chippewa Valley nearly every day, you eventually notice something. Many of the images show scruffy men in work clothes and boots standing around in the snow with lunch plates in hand. Time after time, a round-faced man with a bristly mustache appears among them.

Meet Oluf Sherman. If you worked in a Chippewa Valley lumber camp around the turn of the twentieth century, chances are you ran across the man from time to time. He shows up in at least ten different lumber camp photos in the Chippewa Valley Museum's collections. In my work as archivist for the museum, I've learned to check for his distinctive face in the crowd whenever I run across a new photo from the camps.

Sherman, son of Norwegian immigrants, came to Eau Claire with his family in 1874, at about age five. He apprenticed to jeweler George F. Duncan when he was eleven years old, spent several years working for John Holt on Galloway Street after that and by 1898 had his own business at 205 North Barstow. In 1902, he moved his shop to 217 South Barstow, where it remained until 1930. Oluf's specialty was selling and repairing watches, and lumber camps provided a captive market for him.

The motto of Sherman's business was "quick sales, small profit." He believed he could make more money that way. As a bonus, "the lower prices and smaller profits makes friends for him," according to a 1908 advertisement. The ad summed up his skills by saying, "The watch that he cannot fix and make go is not worth fixing."

Logging crew eating lunch, with Oluf Sherman in long fur coat in foreground, circa 1890–1900. *Courtesy Chippewa Valley Museum.*

The Sherman family, 1910. *Courtesy Chippewa Valley Museum.*

Eau Claire Symphony Orchestra, with Oluf Sherman playing string bass at far left. *Courtesy Chippewa Valley Museum.*

When he wasn't peddling his wares in the woods or working in his shop on Barstow, Oluf was a family man and a musician. He and his wife, Matilda, had eight children—Oliver, Irvin, Bert, Victor, Irma, Hazel, Gordon and Sylvia. Lois Barland, in one of her histories of Eau Claire, calls Oluf an expert musician and mentions that all eight of his kids were musicians as well. Oluf played the bass viola in the Grand Opera House orchestra for many years. He appears in a good half dozen images in the museum's collection of orchestra photos, too.

On December 22, 1929, Oluf sang in a Christmas cantata with the choir at Grace Lutheran Church. His unmistakable face shows up in the middle of the fourth row in a newspaper photo announcing the concert. As it turns out, that was the last time a camera captured a photo of him that would circulate throughout the Chippewa Valley. Oluf Sherman died of pneumonia on January 4, 1930, just less than two weeks after the performance. His obituary the next day included a portrait of him. After that, his face faded from Chippewa Valley memory—until it was rediscovered nine decades later among those sweaty young lumberjacks in the Northwoods.

Chapter 17
DARIUS BRESEE'S BATH

by Jodi Kiffmeyer

Imagine it's 1896 and you're a proper lady crossing the Madison Street bridge over the Chippewa River with your equally proper lady friends. You look down and see a pillar of your community, a man known for his wealth and generosity, bathing on the west bank of the Chippewa River in the nude. At least it looks like he's nude. It's hard to tell for sure.

You go home and tell your husband, who tells Officer Frank Nugent of the Eau Claire Police Department, who goes to the river to investigate and finds a crowd of people gathered around Darius Bresee. By that time, Bresee's out of the water and chasing a group of boys who are throwing rocks at him. Officer Nugent notifies Mr. Bresee he must appear in court to answer the charge of violating a city ordinance against indecent exposure.

The *Eau Claire Daily Leader*, in its reporting of the incident, published an imaginary conversation between the scandalized ladies:

> *"Oh look at that! What a funny animal. I believe it is a sea-serpent!"* [said the first woman].
> *"Where! Where! I don't see anything," said another.*
> *"Oh! I see it, why as I live, it's a mermaid," said the third.*
> *Just then the object of all these exclamations emerged still further from the mad, rushing waters. "A m-e-r-m-a-i-d," echoed the fourth fair dame. "Why, no, it isn't a mermaid. It's a merman."*

Newspaper articles covering the trial carried a similar tone. One was published under the mildly naughty subtitle "Bather as seen from Madison Street bridge—one leg is longer than it really ought to be." To most of the town, the whole thing was a welcome joke. Bresee was a wealthy and prominent man, hardly the kind of person who needed protection from a scandal of this sort.

Bresee brought his bathing suit to court. All accounts agree that it was little more than a "long undershirt" made of gauze, the kind of thing that doesn't leave much to the imagination when wet. Bresee claimed that the Eau Claire shop woman who sold it to him assured him it was what all the fine gentlemen were wearing to the beach that year. He also noted that the ordinance in question forbade nude bathing during the "hours of daylight" and reasoned that he changed into his bathing suit a full four minutes after sundown. Plus, he'd set up two "shingle blocks" to screen him from nosy gossips on the bridge above when he changed out of his street clothes.

Article about Darius Bresee from the *Chicago Tribune*, August 24, 1896. *Public domain, courtesy Newspapers.com.*

Bresee's defense didn't convince Judge Bartlett, who fined him $1 plus $17.06 in court costs (about $670 in 2023). He paid his fine immediately after the trial from a large roll of bills. However, as he counted out the money, he muttered that the case was brought against him out of spite. The people of Chippewa Falls seemed to agree with him. An article in the *Chippewa Herald* called the trial a "travesty of justice" and scolded Eau Claire for poking fun at an "eccentric individual" who had donated more to charity than any other man in the city. The editors included a sarcastic parting shot at the rival city downriver: "[The jurors] might serve notice on lumbermen that hereafter undressed lumber will not be permitted on that portion of the Chippewa river within the corporate limits of the painfully modest Sawdust city."

The people of Eau Claire had a long memory for Bresee's bath. They began calling it the Crime of '96, and newspapers around the country carried tales about the incident. Every time Bresee's name came up in the news for the next several months, it was accompanied by a tongue-in-cheek reference to the event. For example, the following February, he attended a city council meeting to discuss Eau Claire's struggle to supply clean water to residents. Councilman Thomas Frawley remarked that "the water question was indeed important, but, as far as bathing purposes were concerned, the Chippewa River was good enough." Over sixty years later, Lois Barland resurrected the story in *Sawdust City*, her history of early Eau Claire: "[Darius Bresee] was probably best remembered for a bathing incident in 1897 [*sic*] which made headlines for days."

Bresee held a good-natured grudge—against prosecuting attorney Joseph Singleton in particular. Nearly a year after the trial, he took a small bit of revenge. In July 1897, the *Leader* published an article about the residents of Duck Lane, an alley that ran between Farwell and Barstow Streets downtown. They were in an uproar over the rumor that a local lawyer had thrown himself into the Chippewa River in a suicide attempt. Investigation revealed that the "lawyer" was a large snapping turtle that Darius Bresee had captured, confined to Duck Alley and named after a prominent man of the city. The turtle had escaped, and gossip confused the reptile with his namesake.

Who was the turtle named for? A clue turns up five years later, in a newspaper article about local man Charlie Winger, who fished a twenty-pound snapper out of Half Moon Lake. The animal had the initials J.W.S. carved into its shell in honor of Joseph W. Singleton, former city prosecutor.

Chapter 18

CHINESE IMMIGRANTS IN EAU CLAIRE

by Jodi Kiffmeyer

No one would be surprised to hear that immigration has been an issue in Eau Claire since the time the first French priests and fur traders came into the area. Even before that, the Ojibwe were migrants to the Chippewa Valley, following a prophecy that instructed them to move from the eastern part of the continent west to a land where food grew on water. They made their homes where they found *manoomin*, also known as wild rice.

What's changed most about the people seeking homes in Eau Claire has been where they come from. Norwegian, Bohemian, German, Polish and Irish immigrants have well-established histories in the Chippewa Valley. What most people don't know about is the presence of Chinese immigrants in historic Eau Claire.

A brief article in the *Eau Claire Leader* from 1905 gives us a glimpse of how European immigrants and their descendants viewed their counterparts coming from China. It reports the arrival of Inspector R.F. Davis from St. Paul, who was "in the city today on business." His business was investigating the half dozen or so Chinese immigrants who resided in Eau Claire at the time, compelling them to show certificates proving they had permission to live in the United States. He had the law to back him up. The Chinese Exclusion Act of 1882, the first significant immigration law in the United States, banned almost all Chinese people from entering the country. The act was extended in 1892 and made permanent in 1902, along with the new requirement that Chinese people already living in the United States must carry a permit to prove they were in the country legally. A few weeks prior to his visit to Eau Claire, Davis had arrested two Chinese men in Ashland on suspicion they'd been smuggled over the Canadian border.

Most of the Chinese men in Eau Claire (and they were almost certainly men—few Chinese women were allowed to enter the United States at the time) had their papers in order. Only one of the six couldn't show he had permission to be in the country. According to him, he secured a certificate on arriving in St. Paul in 1885 but lost it a few years ago in Eau Claire. He promised to replace it to avoid deportation.

Almost all early Chinese immigrants in Eau Claire worked in the laundry or restaurant industries. George Quong Kee was an example of a man who owned both kinds of businesses. He first appeared in city directories in 1896, operating a laundry on Madison Street. Between 1904 and 1908, Quong Kee owned a few different laundries on North Barstow Street. In 1913, he ventured into the restaurant business, when he and his partner Charley Wing bought the OK Café, a "chop suey house," at 308 Eau Claire Street. In February 1916, Quong Kee became the sole proprietor of the Canton Café, located above a cigar shop at 203 South Barstow Street.

The Canton Café had a bit of a rough reputation from the start. Maybe some of the rowdier elements of Eau Claire thought they could get away with mischief at a place owned by a minority. Whatever it was, there were at least four brushes with the law at the café in its first ten months of operation. All but one involved arrests of patrons who did things like throw food at each other or steal from the till. Quong Kee's one reported infraction was violating a labor law that restricted the number of hours and how late into the evening a woman could work.

In 1917, Eau Claire voters considered a referendum prohibiting alcohol in the city. The *Eau Claire Leader* reported on April 6 that "two prominent and well known businessmen in the eighth ward" had sworn affidavits that Quong Kee was a United States citizen and therefore entitled to vote. It happened that these two men were on the "wet" side of the alcohol question and wanted to help their side along by ingratiating themselves to a hopeful voter. Election workers challenged their statements on the basis that "an alien cannot become a citizen of the United States and cannot vote." The 1882 act denied citizenship to any Chinese individual who might seek it. Quong Kee was turned away from the polls.

Quong Kee's obituary says he left Eau Claire around 1920 and worked in the laundry business in Minneapolis for thirty-seven years. Eau Claire must have meant something to him, though, because he returned there in 1959

Grave of George Quong Kee, 2024. *Courtesy Jodi Kiffmeyer.*

to live with a couple named Simon and Lena Erickson on Second Avenue. The city remained his home until his death in 1966, and he was buried in Lakeview Cemetery.

While Quong Kee was away in Minneapolis, another young Chinese immigrant arrived in Eau Claire, one whose American name eventually became a household word in the city. Chee Yat "Jimmy" Woo, the descendent of a long line of Chinese chefs, came to the United States in 1926 and was cooking in Eau Claire at the Man-Dar-Inn restaurant on Highway 12 by 1935. For over fifteen years—with several months away in 1942 and 1943, serving in the U.S. Army—Woo worked as head chef in half a dozen restaurants in Eau Claire. His cooking became so popular that the White House Inn was advertising it every day in the local newspaper during the mid- to late 1940s.

Jimmy Woo started working for himself in 1950, when he built a restaurant known as Woo's Pagoda on Hastings Way. The establishment became a legend in Eau Claire and surrounding communities, the eighteen-foot wooden pagoda on its roof serving as a landmark on one of the busiest roads in town. Woo decorated the interior Chinese-style, including a replica of the wishing well from his hometown of Kaiping, Guangdong Province.

For all those years in Eau Claire, Jimmy Woo was without most of his family. He arrived in the United States with his father but had to leave

Jimmy Woo's Pagoda Restaurant, circa 1960s. *Courtesy Chippewa Valley Museum.*

behind his wife, Lie Fong, and two sons. In 1952, his son Gam Dong "Don" joined him in Eau Claire, but because of immigration quotas, the rest of the family had to wait. It wasn't until 1962 that Woo was able to bring Lie Fong to the United States for the first time. They'd been married for nearly forty years and had spent only two of those years together.

Although Woo retired in 1978 and died in 1982, his legacy long outlived him. Woo's Pagoda continued operating until 2008, under two different owners. The building was razed in 2014, but a group of concerned citizens salvaged the pagoda, which as of this writing is being restored by a private owner.

Chapter 19

BIG SAUL BRACKETT

by Jodi Kiffmeyer

Saul Brackett, a farmer's son from Elk Mound, made a deal early in the 1900s. If he saved $500 toward tuition at the University of Wisconsin, his father, Abraham, would match it. Education was so important to Saul that he, who turned twenty years old in 1900, was willing to sit in classes with teenagers. Saul's sister Jennie left for the Normal School in Stevens Point in 1902, and he went along with her to enroll in the town's high school. During his year there, he was a star football player and earned one of the first athletic letters given away by the school.

In 1903, the City of Eau Claire assembled a group of young men it hoped would take the town to the high school state football championships. To bolster the teenagers from Eau Claire, coaches recruited a group of "strong men" from surrounding rural areas, including "Big Sol Brackett" at right tackle. Coaches prepared the team for the state competition by scheduling a tough lineup of opponents, including teams from Minneapolis, Madison and Chicago. Eau Claire did go on to win the state championship that year, though their final opponent, Fort Atkinson, boycotted the game in protest of a venue change.

When he wasn't playing football, Saul delivered the *Eau Claire Leader* on South Barstow Street, the longest route in the city. In the summer, he earned money by hiring out as a farmhand, working on the railroad and lumberjacking. In this last endeavor, Saul followed in the boot prints of hundreds of other men in the Chippewa Valley, including his father and brother, who went to work in the woods and on the water bringing logs to the mills in Chippewa Falls and Eau Claire.

Little Falls Dam near Holcombe, about the time of Saul Brackett's drowning. *Courtesy Chippewa Valley Museum.*

One Friday morning in July 1905, word arrived in Eau Claire that the Chippewa Lumber and Boom Company needed help breaking up a logjam at the Little Falls Dam near Holcombe. Saul saw an opportunity to make money—perhaps enough to meet his $500 goal at last. He joined more than seventy other men on a train leaving Eau Claire at 7:45 a.m. and arrived at the dam just over an hour later.

The men went right to work loading themselves and their tools into batteaux, canoe-like boats used by lumbering crews to navigate the jams. Foreman Walter Sugars ordered the drivers to form crews of ten men, the typical limit for one batteau. However, when Sugars left the riverbank briefly, sixteen men crowded into one boat. Witnesses reported that the sides of the batteau barely cleared the surface of the river, even in calm water. The crew navigated to the center of the river toward the jam but were unable to make a safe landing. Instead, the rush of water carried them downstream. Three men jumped to the safety of the piled logs before the boat capsized, but the rest weren't as lucky. Saul found himself among those who were struggling in the rapids to save their lives. Witnesses could hear him encouraging one of his fellow swimmers before he disappeared into the froth.

Four men sprang into a batteau to rescue their friends. They, too, capsized but were able to swim to safety. The following day, searchers closed the dam, hoping to lower the water enough to retrieve what they knew would be dead bodies. They recovered Saul a mile and a half downstream from the dam. In all, eleven men died that day, in what is possibly the worst drowning disaster in Chippewa River history.

The accident cast a shadow over Eau Claire, particularly the loss of Saul. He was a member of Company E of the Wisconsin National Guard, so when news of his death reached Chippewa Falls, Captain E.S. Pearsall drove his car—probably one of only a few in town in those years—to Elk Mound to notify the family. Abraham Brackett made his way to Little Falls and was there to receive Saul's body when searchers found it.

Local newspapers memorialized Saul in article after article. The *Eau Claire Leader* praised the work he did delivering papers for them: "The young man was most thorough and fewer complaints were registered from the patrons along the route handled by young Brackett than any in the experience of the *Leader*." Saul's funeral was reportedly larger than any in Elk Mound history up to that point. The church could hold only half of the crowd, and the procession to Waneka Cemetery stretched for over a mile and a half. Saul was buried next to his mother, who died before he was old enough to remember her. His fellow soldiers from Company E saluted him with three volleys of gunfire and played taps as mourners left the graveside.

To add to the tragedy, Saul's bank notified his father that he'd reached a balance of $500 in his account the day before his death. He could have stayed safely at home. Had Saul Brackett survived, he would have graduated from Eau Claire High School in December that year and gone off to Madison to pursue the education he worked so hard for.

Chapter 20

FAAST'S MADE-TO-ORDER FARMS

by Jodi Kiffmeyer

Once the logging companies had stripped the land of every useful tree, they faced the question of what to do with what was left. That land in the northern part of Wisconsin became known as the cutover. Some landowners stopped paying taxes and abandoned the land. Others formed or used the services of colonization companies that actively sought to bring settlers to the cutover land in the first three decades of the twentieth century.

The most innovative ideas for Wisconsin's cutover land came from the mind of Ben Faast, son of Albert Faast, a shoemaker and lifelong resident of Eau Claire. Ben started out with very little. His father suffered from a mysterious illness that baffled doctors and died without warning in 1897, when Ben was in his early teens. Frances, Ben's mother, had to sell off Albert's stock of shoes and his tools to cover the family's bills. Despite her best efforts, the Faasts' house was foreclosed on a few months later.

Before Ben entered the business, the idea of developing land meant selling it to whomever would buy it for whatever they could think to do with it. Faast saw that the standards of living in other regions of Wisconsin had risen so high that settlers wouldn't be content to endure the same hardships as pioneers of earlier days. He believed that by adding value to the land first, in the form of good roads and planned towns, he could make a better profit and interact with the incoming settlers in a more ethical way.

In 1917, Faast and two partners incorporated the Wisconsin Colonization Company and purchased around fifty thousand acres of land in Sawyer

County. With the land, the company planned to put into practice one of Faast's most innovative ideas: the "made-to-order farm." This package consisted of forty acres of cutover land, a house (buyer's choice from four plans), livestock and enough wire to fence ten acres. To pay the cost, settlers put down 20 percent in cash but didn't have to make any other payments during the first three years if they lived on and developed their land. After that, they had thirty years to pay off the mortgage.

The Wisconsin Colonization Company found other ways to support farmers as well. It helped them access affordable credit for improving their land. The company owned a farm that kept livestock on hand to sell to farmers and developed seeds that would grow in the difficult climate of the northern part of the state. A formally trained farmer taught settlers seientifically tested methods that extended the benefits of research done at the University of Wisconsin in Madison. The company laid out roads and tested land to find soil that would best support agriculture. This last benefit was important to Faast, who told others in the company, "We must never sell a piece of land to anyone unless we ourselves believe that it can be developed into a successful farm as the man dreams who is buying it."

Possibly the most ambitious of Faast's ventures was the town of Ojibwa along the Chippewa River in Sawyer County. Faast planned Ojibwa with the help of Professors Leonard Smith and Franz Aust from the University

Conrath, Wisconsin: an advertisement for a stump-pulling demonstration on a Faast farm, 1911. *Courtesy Chippewa Valley Museum.*

90

of Wisconsin, specialists in city planning and landscape design. They laid out streets, parks and community gardens, reserving space for a courthouse and an agricultural school. Strict zoning laws required all buildings to be white and in the colonial style. A part of town was reserved for wealthier people, where houses had to cost at least a certain amount. By 1921, Ojibwa boasted a railroad station, a school, several businesses and a newspaper—the *Ojibwa Courier*—published by Faast. Although the family maintained their home in Eau Claire, Ben; his wife, Ida; and their daughter, Margaret, spent summers in Ojibwa.

Faast's connections with the university in Madison ran deep. He was personal friends with President Charles Van Hise and H.L. Russell, dean of the College of Agriculture. He was on the board of regents from 1914 to 1932 and used his influence to encourage and enable the sons of settlers in his colonies to pursue an education at the university. He was vice president and director of the Federal Land Bank in St. Paul from 1917 to 1928. In other words, Faast had the connections to make his plans for northern Wisconsin work if they could.

Unfortunately, the land held too many obstacles to bring large numbers of settlers into the area. Short growing seasons aside, a backbreaking task confronted newcomers from the moment they took possession of their land, something implied in the word *cutover*: they had to remove stumps from enough land to grow crops. Faast worked with the University of Wisconsin and other real estate developers in the Chippewa Valley to find solutions to this problem. They brought "Land Clearing Special" trains to small towns in the area with tools and stump-pulling demonstrations. The government provided surplus World War I dynamite in hopes of expediting the process. Even the dynamite wasn't enough to reclaim land that, according to returning soldiers who tried their luck at farming, looked like the World War I battlefields of Europe.

The hoped-for town of Ojibwa never became what Faast thought it could be. He was there at his summer home on the afternoon of June 10, 1948, when he suffered a heart attack. Two days later, an ambulance from Ladysmith brought him to Luther Hospital in Eau Claire, and he died there on June 14. His daughter, Margaret, graduated from the University of Wisconsin just a few days later.

Chapter 21

CLYDE VAN GORDEN: EAU CLAIRE'S INVENTOR

by Diana Peterson

C lyde Schuyler Van Gorden was a true Renaissance man, inventing several products during his lifetime. He was born in Hixton, Wisconsin, in 1892, the youngest of five siblings. His parents were in their forties at that time. In 1912, he married Elsie Charlotte Caley in Racine, Wisconsin. Van Gorden went to business college in Winona for two years and then spent a year at UW Madison studying electrical engineering. Clyde's father was a merchant in Osseo who owned five stores.

Van Gorden's first invention was a dust mop. The head, used for furniture dusting, could be removed, cleaned and replaced if necessary. He sold more than one hundred thousand of them in the early 1920s.

In 1923, Clyde started a radio station in Osseo, Wisconsin, WTAQ. He built his own transmitting equipment. After two years, he sold it to Gillette Rubber Co. in Eau Claire. The radio station, which the company purchased to help with advertising, started out in the Gillette cafeteria and later was set up at Hotel Eau Claire. Jim Franey was hired as general manager and advertising salesman. Two announcers were also hired: Bill Curtz and Bill Kline. Curtz was also the studio operator and played phonographs, and Kline was the newscaster. In 1928, WTAQ joined the Columbia Broadcasting System, which later became CBS.

In 1932, Gillette sold the station to St. Norbert University in Green Bay, and the call letters went to a radio station in Illinois. Eau Claire was left without a radio station until 1937, when WEAU went on the air.

After getting to know Van Gorden, Gillette hired him as its sales manager, a job he did from 1928 to 1939. As a manager, he traveled around the Midwest. One day, when he was in Aberdeen, South Dakota, he heard about a new marine-grade plywood and stopped by to check it out; he must have liked the product because he bought a train carload of it.

Now he needed a plan for the wood, so Clyde decided to go into business with Olsen Bait Company owner R.C. Olsen. They created a revolutionary fishing boat. The factory was in the Gotzian Shoe Building in Chippewa Falls. The plan was to produce ten boats a day during the winter and up to fifty a day by spring. They made two kinds of boats: the Chippewa Chief and the Chippewa Scout. The Chief was more of a sport boat and weighed seventy-five pounds, while the Scout was an open boat, weighing in at seventy pounds. It was easy for one person to launch the lightweight boats, and they could be mounted on top of a car for transporting. Both models were waterproof and watertight, making them sturdier than an ordinary boat and able to float on top of the water. Their special construction made them vibrationless with any type of outboard motor. Prior to this, the boats' material was used exclusively by airplane manufacturers for wing and fuselage construction. In addition, both models featured an M stern to prevent skidding and a streamlined keel. The boats required little upkeep; they never needed caulking, only an occasional paint job.

Van Gorden realized that building a boat with nails instead of screws was more practical because nails provided seven hundred pounds of pressure while screws only provided two hundred. The industry had decided only screws were acceptable, but instead of giving up, Van Gorden educated his sales distributors and demonstrated the difference between the construction methods.

In 1939, the boat company moved to Eau Claire, where it continued to build 1,500 to 2,000 boats per year. The name of the company changed to CS Van Gorden and Son. By the '50s, there were twenty-five different styles to choose from. The company employed seven factory representatives who sold the boats to eight hundred different distributors. It also made a twelve-foot paddle board for lifesaving on public beaches and a six-foot surfboard. In 1966, the company put out its anchor and closed down. During his time making boats, Van Gorden was given seven patents for boat designs and inventions.

In 1939, Van Gorden had another idea for using that marine plywood. He had considered building prefab homes, but the one issue he faced in designing them was preventing ice buildup. One morning, Clyde woke up with an idea and ran to his shop to check it out. His idea was to build screen vents that he placed under the eaves of the house, which circulated air in the attic, preventing ice from building up on the roof. Van Gorden mentioned in an interview with the *Leader Telegram* in June 1972 that he was the first person to receive a federal house loan for this type of home. An inspector came to check it out because he could not believe Van Gorden had found a way to get around the ice buildup. In 1940, Van Gorden rolled out his first house for his own family to occupy, a single-story, two-bedroom home with a basement that cost $2,150. Labor costs for this type of construction were only $400. The houses, called Van-Homes, were in production until 1962. Van Gorden built

Portrait of Clyde Van Gorden, date unknown. *Courtesy Chippewa Valley Museum.*

about 1,200 of them, 400 in Eau Claire. The most expensive house was $9,000, and it was a story and a half with three bedrooms.

In his spare time, Van Gorden also invented several types of cement, a crack-proof plaster that stuck to almost everything, and a sealer with a rubber base to use on boats and other items. His last big project was the invention of Van's Instant Gun Blue, which removes grease and rust and blues steel. The company had sold two million of them by 1955. At that time, the kit cost one dollar. The price has increased since that time, but it's still available today and can be purchased from most sporting goods stores.

During World War II, Van Gorden worked for the Small Business Corporation in Chicago. He was also a civic leader, serving on the Eau Claire City Council for two years. He was a sports enthusiast and also belonged to several organizations, including the Elks and the Masons. Van Gorden died on May 9, 1975, and is buried at Forest Hill Cemetery.

Clyde Van Gorden was a true pioneer in several fields and worked hard to develop new and improved products and ways of doing business.

Chapter 22

THERE'S A NEW SHERIFF IN TOWN

by Diana Peterson

Westerns were very popular in the 1950s. Being a sheriff was seen as a dangerous occupation and garnered a lot of respect.

In the early '50s, NBC reported that 3,181 families in Eau Claire owned a television. The city got an early Christmas gift on December 23, 1953, when WEAU began airing television shows. The station featured programs from NBC, ABC and Dumont. The day it debuted, you could tune in to watch *Hopalong Cassidy*, championship wrestling, a Christmas special, *Theater Thirteen* and, of course, the news and weather.

The following year, Bob Dawson arrived in Eau Claire from Des Moines and joined WEAU as an announcer and meteorologist. Dawson, born in 1924, grew up in Des Moines before enrolling at Drake University and then the American Institute of the Air, studying radio broadcasting. Bob served in the army during World War II as an artillery sergeant and received the Bronze Star. After the war, he went to work for Des Moines television station KCBC.

In 1955, Dawson took on the persona of Sheriff Bob, which he had first created in Iowa. Until 1978, he entertained kids on *The Sheriff Bob Show*. He had a quick wit and an outgoing personality that the kids were drawn to. The show aired on Thursdays at 4:30, with a live audience—including lots of Scout groups, birthday party guests and neighborhood friends. Residents tuned in to see Bob as well as their friends and family who might be there in person. Audience members remember being in awe of the lights and cameras.

Sheriff Bob visiting hospitalized children, circa 1965. *Courtesy Chippewa Valley Museum.*

Outfitted in full cowboy gear, Dawson talked with the kids, taught them important life lessons and served as a role model. He and his friend Colonel Larson from the Wausau area often did tricks for the kids. The audience sat on bleachers and got to enjoy hot dogs and chocolate milk during cartoons. There were special guests and prizes.

Parents would contact the station so Sheriff Bob could wish their kids a happy birthday or tell them to feel better when they were sick. Just bring up the name Sheriff Bob around a bunch of baby boomers at a function in Eau Claire and the stories go on and on.

In his personal time, Dawson donned his western gear and went to visit kids at the local hospital. Both patients and caregivers were grateful for the time he spent with them. Nurses told tales about children doing things for Sheriff Bob that they wouldn't do for the nurses, including getting shots and eating their meals. Dawson called himself a "frustrated doctor who was happy to do whatever he could to help whether it was reading books or taking a walk."

In 1973, Bob was honored with the first Award for Humanitarian Accomplishments by the Tri-County Medical Society. Eau Claire County named Dawson an honorary sheriff in 2007. After ninety full years, the sheriff passed away in 2014.

Dawson was proud of his badge. After someone borrowed his and lost it, Eau Claire sheriff Ron Cramer supplied Bob with a new one. Kids respected it. After Senator Robert Kennedy was murdered in 1968, Bob's wife told him it was probably time for him to hang up his guns. Both of his arms had been given to him: one was a gas-operated BB gun, and the other was a .22-caliber revolver. He had carried them for thirteen years, but he knew she was right. He said kids didn't even notice, but they were quick to point out he wasn't wearing his badge the day he left it at home.

Chippewa Valley Community Television did a three-part documentary about Dawson, *Sheriff Bob*, and it's fun to listen to the memories people shared about their time with the sheriff. Two of the interviewees captured what Bob meant to the City of Eau Claire. Tami Schraufnagel said that the show "is a piece of Eau Claire history, and Bob Dawson deserves every bit of acclaim that he can possibly have for being Sheriff Bob…It was the *Captain Kangaroo* of Eau Claire." Rob Mattison recalled meeting Dawson as an adult. He said, "I was really starstruck. I don't get that starstruck by national stars that I do with this man.…I just still think he's the biggest star Eau Claire has ever had."

Sheriff Bob is remembered and appreciated for the joy he brought to kids every week on his show for decades, but he is revered and loved even more for the joy he brought to hospitalized children for so many years.

Chapter 23

WISCONSIN'S MR. BASEBALL

by Diana Peterson

Baseball has always held a special place in Eau Claire's heart. In the 1860s, when there were three "base ball" teams, games were well attended. Eau Claire claimed a Class C minor league baseball team from 1933 to 1962. Beginning as an affiliate of the Chicago Cubs, the team later represented the Boston Braves. When the Braves moved to Milwaukee in the 1950s, the Eau Claire Bears became the Eau Claire Braves. The team enjoyed a lot of success, winning numerous pennants and hosting players who would go on to be stars in the majors. Most people know that Hank Aaron, Bill Bruton and Joe Torre played in Eau Claire—but if you were an Eau Claire Braves fan in 1956 and 1957, you would have had a chance to watch Bob Uecker in action.

Born in 1936 in Milwaukee, Uecker was a hometown boy. His father immigrated from Switzerland in 1923. Bob enjoyed riding his bike to Borchert Field to watch his favorite baseball players. He played basketball and baseball in high school.

At age twenty, Bob enlisted in the U.S. Army, hoping to play baseball for the military. At the time, he had never played in the minors or in college, which was a requirement to get on the team. Never one to let a little fact get in the way, he claimed he had played ball at Marquette. Little did Uecker know that Marquette did not have a baseball team, but neither did any of the military brass, who never followed up on his claim to fame, so he made the team. He played at Fort Leonard Wood in Missouri and at Fort Belvoir in Virginia.

Bob Uecker as an Eau Claire Brave, 1957. *Courtesy Chippewa Valley Museum.*

After his discharge, Uecker was signed by the Milwaukee Braves as a catcher in 1956 for $3,000. He bounced around the minors for six years, playing in Eau Claire for the first two. Bob played under managers Joe Just in 1956 and Gordon Maltzberger in 1957. During those years, the team finished the season with seventy wins both years and fifty-two losses in 1956 and fifty-five losses in 1957. In 1956, the team went to the playoffs, losing to the Duluth Superior White Sox.

There is no end to the stories about Uecker during his time in Eau Claire. One day, he showed up at practice in a straw hat, long underwear and bib overalls because that's what he threw in his bag when the uniforms were laundered. One of his teammates shared that one night, several of them went to a local bar. A very large man came in with a beautiful woman. When the man went to the restroom, Uecker said he was going to kiss the woman. His friends tried to talk him out of it, but he did it anyway. Of course, the man returned and saw Uecker kissing her. His friends went to help him out, only to learn that the woman was Bob's wife, and he'd set up the entire thing.

After leaving Eau Claire, Uecker moved on to minor league teams in Boise, Atlanta, Jacksonville, Wichita, Indianapolis and finally Louisville, after which time he was moved up to the major leagues with the Milwaukee Braves in 1962. While Bob's career began to flourish in 1962, the year was not as kind to the Eau Claire Braves, whose team folded due to decreasing attendance. From 1962 to '67, Bob was a backup catcher with the Milwaukee Braves, the St. Louis Cardinals, the Philadelphia Phillies and the Atlanta Braves.

During his six seasons as a major league catcher, Uecker batted .200, getting 146 hits and scoring 14 home runs. Uecker joked about two highlights of his career: "when he walked with bases loaded to drive in the winning run in an intersquad game during spring training" and when he "hit a home run off future Hall of Famer Sandy Koufax," although he said he "feared that home run would keep Koufax from getting into the Hall of Fame."

After retiring, Bob kept busy. In 1971, he was hired as a play-by-play announcer for the Milwaukee Brewers during their second year in Milwaukee. Uecker became "the voice of the Brewers," providing humor for fans whether the team was winning or losing with his quick wit and self-deprecating comments. He told a lot of stories, like one about the time he hit a grand slam off Ron Herbel. Bob said that "when the manager came out to get Ron, he was bringing Herbel's suitcase." He also commented that "sporting goods companies would pay me not to endorse their products."

Uecker became a fixture on the *Tonight Show*, making more than one hundred appearances. Johnny Carson, the host, dubbed him Mr. Baseball.

From 1985 to 1990, Uecker starred in *Mr. Belvedere* as George Owens, a sportswriter. One night on Johnny Carson, talking about his acting career, Uecker said, "Even when I played baseball, I was acting."

Uecker is also well-known for his role of play-by-play announcer Harry Doyle on the big screen in *Major League* and its two sequels. One of his catchphrases came from this role. To downplay a wild pitch, he described it as "juuust a bit outside." Uecker is also remembered for his Miller Lite commercials.

Bob Uecker has been honored with many awards during his life. He was inducted into the National Radio Hall of Fame in 2001, and in 2003, he received the Ford C. Frick Award for his broadcasting career. In 2005, his fiftieth anniversary in baseball, the Brewers honored him by placing the number 50 in the Ring of Honor, near the retired numbers of Robin Yount and Paul Molitor. In 2012, the Brewers placed the Uecker Monument outside the field, alongside statues of Hank Aaron, Robin Yount and Bud Selig.

Wisconsin governor Tony Evers declared September 25, 2021, Bob Uecker Day to celebrate his fiftieth year in baseball broadcasting. Brewer fans have enjoyed listening to him on the radio for fifty-three of the club's fifty-four years in Milwaukee.

In addition to baseball, Uecker spent some time with World Wrestling Entertainment, and he was inducted into the Celebrity Wing of the WWE Hall of Fame in 2010 for his appearances in WrestleMania III and IV.

Uecker can also add "author" to his résumé. He published an autobiography in 1984, *Catcher in the Wry: Outrageous but True Stories of Baseball*.

According to a 2011 *Leader Telegram* article by John Casper Jr., "Bob doesn't remember the name of the drug store where he bought his bats or the bar where he enjoyed burgers and beer, but he said 'Eau Claire's a great town. That was a good time in my life.'" Bob said, "The Northern League was a good league. And there were a lot of good ball players to come out of Eau Claire." However, he did not love the road trips.

The 2011 *Leader Telegram* article quoted Uecker as saying, "I have many fond memories of Eau Claire." Eau Claire is grateful for all the fond memories Bob Uecker gave us also. Who knew that the gangly kid who came to Eau Claire in 1956 would be a state icon almost seventy years later?

Chapter 24

JOHN MYHERS: FROM ROME TO *THE TWILIGHT ZONE*

by Diana Peterson

If you watched television in the '60s, you would recognize John Myhers. Myhers, known locally as Jack, was born in Strum, Wisconsin, in 1921 and grew up in Eau Claire. He began singing at the age of twelve, and he won several national contests. He took on several leading roles with the St. Paul Civic Opera while attending the MacPhail School of Music.

William S. MacPhail, an original member of the Minnesota Orchestra, founded the MacPhail School of Violin in 1907. It expanded soon after, becoming the MacPhail School of Music and Dramatic Art and moving to a four-story facility. After MacPhail's death, the family gifted the school, along with its one hundred faculty members and three thousand students, to the University of Minnesota. MacPhail has worked with a variety of musicians from Lawrence Welk to Prince.

At MacPhail, Myhers studied under instructors James and Sylva Manley. (James grew up in Menomonie, Wisconsin.) A local Eau Claire voice teacher commented in the *Leader Telegram* that "it's unusual to find a student singer so possessed of the poise and musical confidence that John Myhers displayed."

During World War II, John joined the army and served in Italy. There, he began writing, staging and singing in shows for soldiers. He loved Italy so much that he stayed there for eleven years after his discharge. He studied opera and took courses in filmmaking. Myhers spent time studying at the American Academy and earned a doctoral degree in literature from the

University of Rome. While learning his craft, he appeared in a variety of Roman films and received a small part in *Quo Vadis* when it was shot on location there.

Quo Vadis was a 1951 religious epic film set in ancient Rome during Emperor Nero's reign. It was filmed in Technicolor and nominated for eight Oscars. The film was such a big box office success that it was credited with single-handedly rescuing Metro-Goldwyn-Mayer from bankruptcy.

When a former *Leader Telegram* reporter, Joan Oyass, toured Europe with her parents in 1949, she visited with Myhers in Rome and wrote an article for the paper about his experiences there. He told Oyass that "Eau Claire is the city I like best."

After returning to the United States, Myhers began his acting career on Broadway, touring in *Kiss Me Kate*, *The Golden Fleecing* and *The Good Soup*. He was Captain Von Trapp for four years in the first national touring company of *The Sound of Music* in the early '60s. He also worked with Katharine Hepburn in a Stratford, Connecticut production of *Antony and Cleopatra* and with Jack Lemmon and Charlton Heston in several companies.

Myhers made several appearances on *The Tonight Show* with both Jack Paar and Steve Allen. He also tried his hand at writing, producing the script for a film, *Weddings and Babies*, in 1958.

In 1962, he married Joan Benedict, and they moved to Hollywood the following year. Benedict was born in Brooklyn. She also studied in Rome for some time, at the Opera Ballet School, before living in Paris during her youth. At fifteen, she studied with Stella Adler and Robert Lewis before majoring in drama and speech at Hofstra University. Joan is also an actor, with twenty-four credits to her name on the Internet Movie Database.

Joan had a relationship with Rod Steiger as a young woman, but when she met John, she knew he was the one. They were married for thirty years, until his death. After he passed away, Steiger reconnected with her, and they were married from 2000 to 2002, when Steiger passed away. At age ninety-six, Joan is still doing well.

During his career, John had roles in seventy films, including *History of the World (Part 1)*, *How to Succeed in Business Without Really Trying*, *1776* and *The Shaggy DA*.

In 1968, he was in *The Private Navy of Sergeant O'Farrell* with Gina Lollobrigida, Bob Hope, Jeffrey Hunter and Phyllis Diller. In 1980, he added "director" to his résumé when he wrote and directed *The Prize Fighter* with Don Knotts and Tim Conway. By the end of his career, he had accumulated fifty directing credits.

Ad from the *Leader Telegram* from June 2, 1968, for a John Myhers film. *Courtesy of the* Leader Telegram.

John also started accepting roles on television. His first appearance was in 1958 on *Camera Three*, a weekly examination of the arts and literature. Myhers showed up in many of the most popular shows on the air. You can catch him in reruns on *Alice, Charlie's Angels, Fantasy Island* (six times) *Get Smart* (three times), *High Chaparral, Hogan's Heroes* (four times), *I Dream of Jeannie* (two times), *Love American Style* (seven times), *The Bionic Woman, The Doris Day Show, The Flying Nun, The Mothers-In-Law, The Name of the Game* and *The Waltons*. His last acting role was on *The Twilight Zone* in 1985.

Later in his career, Myhers taught screenwriting at the Film Industry Workshop in Los Angeles, where he wrote a textbook, *The Myhers Method*.

He passed away in 1992 from pneumonia after a fifty-year career as singer, director, teacher, writer and actor. Many articles about him state that he was well-liked in Hollywood, had a great sense of humor and seemed to have a lot of friends who enjoyed spending time with him.

PART IV

ON THE MOVE

Chapter 25

Was Dr. Ashum Crazy to Buy a Locomobile?

by Diana Peterson

While I'm sure David Ashum was a very fine doctor, one of his claims to fame was being the first person to have an automobile in Eau Claire.

Ashum was born in Findlay, Ohio, in 1854. His father was a farmer, and both his parents died when he was young. He apprenticed under Dr. John A. Waterhouse in Bay City, Michigan. In 1881, he enrolled at the Eclectic Medical Institute in Cincinnati. Eclectic medicine made use of botanical remedies for substance abuse and other ailments. The term was coined by Constantine Samuel Ratinesque, a botanist at Transylvania University. The treatments included Native American medicines and purges with calomel and other mercury-based substances, as well as bloodletting.

The Cincinnati School started as the Eclectic Medical Institute in Worthington, Ohio, in 1830. When corpses from a grave robbery were found lying on the medical college's dissection tables in 1839, the public outcry caused the school to lose its state charter. Dr. Beach, the founder, and the entire faculty founded a new Eclectic Medical Institute in Cincinnati. Attendance peaked in the 1880s and 1890s, but by 1939, it was closed.

After receiving his medical degree, Dr. Ashum moved to Bay City, Michigan, where another eclectic colleague had started a hospital to treat loggers. The Bay City Hospital sent Ashum to Stevens Point, Wisconsin, to open a second hospital, and within the year, he was sent to Eau Claire, starting a lumbermen's hospital on South Barstow Street. The three hospitals were managed by the Michigan and Wisconsin Hospital Co. They sold one-year treatment plans for loggers for $7.50. Ashum's colleagues at the hospital were Drs. Lyman, Hayes, Midelfart and Thrane.

Because fires were a common threat to buildings in the mid-1880s, the hospital made sure it was well protected from fire damage. There were seventy-two pails of water in strategic locations around the institution. Standing pipes leading from the steam pumps in the cellar were also easily accessible. The building featured hundreds of feet of hoses and four exits.

Dr. Ashum became one of the first presidents of the Eau Claire Medical Society. He was also a member of the Ancient Free and Accepted Masons.

In 1889, the doctor attended York Polyclinic and was a member of the national and state eclectic medical societies. He was the head of the Narcotic Cure Co. in Eau Claire in 1893.

In May 1901, Dr. Ashum's Locomobile arrived in Eau Claire. It was shipped in parts and had to be assembled. In April, he'd traveled to St. Paul to buy the steam-powered car from Joy Brothers for $800. In 2024, that car would cost about $29,000. It sat two people, went from one to forty miles per hour and had a four- to five-horsepower motor. An attachment shut off the gas when the steam reached 180 pounds of pressure. It must have been a good car, because in September 1901, Ashum's colleague Dr. Lyman also purchased one.

The Locomobile Co. of America Pioneering Co., begun in 1899, was known for its dedication to precision before the assembly-line era. Founded by Amzi L. Barber in 1899 in Watertown, Massachusetts, the company moved to Bridgeport in 1900. From 1899 to 1903, it manufactured affordable small steam cars; after 1903, it produced internal combustion–powered luxury autos. In 1922, it was purchased by Durant Motors. It closed in 1929, as a result of the Great Depression. Its four-story factory was one of the biggest in the world.

J.B. Walker coined the name *Locomobile*—combining *locomotive* and *automobile*—after he bought plans for a steam-powered car from the Stanley brothers for $250,000 (equivalent to $8,794,000 in 2024). Walker sold 50 percent of his partnership to Barber. Their partnership lasted two weeks before Walker left and founded Mobile Co. of America in Tarrytown, New York. In 1903, Samuel Todd Davis Jr., Barber's son-in-law, took over the company.

The first Locomobile had a bicycle framework with a carriage body, a twin cylinder simple engine and a fourteen-inch boiler under the driver's seat. The boiler had to be refilled every twenty miles.

Dr. Lyman took Dr. Ashum's advice and bought a Locomobile, 1901. *Courtesy Chippewa Valley Museum.*

Steam Locomobiles were prone to kerosene fires. Middle-class Americans liked them, especially people who had to travel a lot, like salesmen and doctors. More than four thousand were built between 1899 and 1902. In 1904, a Runabout was created that seated two people and featured a two-cylinder steam engine in a wood-framed car with improved boilers and a new water pump.

A Loco won the 1908 Vanderbilt Cup with a speed of 64.38 miles per hour. The Locomobile factory was near Seaside Park, and the cars were often taken on gravel drives for testing. The Loco was the first car that did not resemble a horse and buggy.

The Gallant Journey was a seven-passenger Loco that debuted in 1911. In 1946, *The Gallant Journey* was a big-screen film. As part of the advance publicity, Columbia Pictures sponsored a cross-country Boston to Los Angeles tour featuring a 1911 Locomobile car.

Andrew Carnegie and Charlie Chaplin both owned Locomobiles. When it came to the luxury-grade Locos, Tiffany and Co. supplied all the silver for the cars.

You might be wondering what the second car Dr. Ashum purchased was: a 1905 Ford Model F, a combination of a Model A and a Model C but larger, more modern and more luxurious. Production ended in 1906 after about one thousand were made.

In June 1901, the *Leader Telegram* announced that a potential race between Dr. Ashum in his Loco and John Hawley on his motorcycle was set for July 4 on the north side hill. I have to say that after learning so much about the Locomobile, I don't think Dr. Ashum was crazy to purchase one, but I can't say I'm as confident about his decision to race against a motorcycle through Eau Claire at the age of forty-seven!

Chapter 26

DRIVING AROUND EAU CLAIRE IN THE 1930s

by Diana Peterson

In 1930, Eau Claire had a population of twenty-six thousand people, and the city was spreading out from its downtown roots. Dr. Ashum bought the first car in Eau Claire in 1901, and by 1930, there were about fifteen dealerships in the city. People obviously enjoyed driving, and there were some interesting stories about driving during this decade.

TIRE TESTING

On December 2, 1930, the *Leader Telegram* reported that Mr. and Mrs. Norman Auer of Eau Claire had completed their task of driving five hundred thousand miles in three and a half years. They were test drivers for Gillette Rubber whose job was to provide information about how well Gillette tires held up. The couple traveled all over the United States, as well as through parts of Canada and Mexico. They shared the driving duty, and during this period, they drove two Chevrolets and five Buicks.

December 9 would see them pulling out of Eau Claire again for San Antonio in a new Studebaker. Going along for the ride were John Skogstad and Palmer Kvisler in a Chevy and Jerry Skogstad and Ernest Fagerland in an International Truck. This time their mission was to drive six hundred miles a day for the winter season through a variety of weather and road conditions.

A gentleman driving on Farwell Street, downtown Eau Claire, in 1930. *Courtesy Chippewa Valley Museum.*

A Different Meaning of "Can I Borrow the Car?"

Allen Klink, seventeen, pled guilty to operating an automobile without the owner's consent in February 1933. Klink had helped himself to a Studebaker coupe that belonged to William Erickson the October before. He and another youth drove the car to Mondovi, where they "borrowed" a Chevrolet, driving both cars to Becky Springs, south of Eau Claire on Highway 37. They left the Studebaker there, bringing the Chevy back to Eau Claire.

Two weeks before his guilty plea, Klink took off with a Chrysler coupe that belonged to Hank Estes. After driving it around town for several hours, he swapped it for Herman Gemmenden's Buick sedan, which he left on the north side hill. To help fund his trip, he also broke a lock at a Chippewa Falls filling station to steal some gasoline. Someone should have told him that there was an easier way to test-drive cars.

Jimmie Burns in Town

In July 1935, stuntman Jimmie Burns arrived in Eau Claire. He had been a stunt driver for fourteen years and held all the official stunt driving records. His plan for the weekend: to drive a car around Eau Claire blindfolded. Chief of police Chris Laursen took a spin with Burns on Friday to ensure that he was a safe driver blindfolded. Burns performed to the chief's satisfaction, so the demonstration was a given a go.

Burns left the Ford garage at two o'clock in the afternoon, driving for an hour and a half around the city and ending up back at the Ford garage. Local volunteers secured his blindfold with tape and inspected the car before and after. Viewers could watch the car on its adventure around town.

Burns claimed that he had never disobeyed any traffic signs or violated any traffic laws during his career. His longest trek blindfolded was from New York to Los Angeles.

Burns and his blindfold had appeared in Eau Claire in 1927, so many people remembered him. He endeared himself to the city by praising local manufacturer Gillette Rubber Co., saying, "Since 1927, every racing car I've driven has been equipped with Gillette tires. I use them for my own safety."

Look Mom, No Hands—or Driver

In October 1935, another stunt car came to town—a phantom one! A driverless car, sponsored by local merchants, made a trip around downtown. A second car drove behind it with a remote control. The route was published in the paper so residents could come see the ghost car as it drove by. Before and after the drive, people were invited to inspect both cars up close at various merchants, including Opheim Sales Co., Sears Roebuck & Co., Webb Oil Co. and Zenith Sales Co.

A Nice Day for a Drive

A different type of driving was reported in the paper by John Huebsch and George Rathbun. One sunny day in 1930 when no caddies were available, they did some driving with their golf clubs. Why were no caddies available? Perhaps because it was early January. When they yelled, "Fore," it was to warn skaters on the rinks that were created on the course in winter. The skaters did not seem amused.

These were not young, mischievous boys. The men were in their fifties and sixties. Huebsch and Rathbun golfed together a lot during their lives, in all types of weather. They also participated in one of Eau Claire's only foxhunts. They oversaw a rabbit-hunting competition for several years. Being members of several fraternal organizations like the Elks also kept them busy. They seemed to have a lot of friends and were mentioned in the *Leader Telegram* as pallbearers together for funerals quite often.

On that specific winter day, the men reported that Rathbun won 45–48 and no balls were lost.

Chapter 27

DRIVE ON IN

by Diana Peterson

I t's the 1950s. You have on your comfiest pajamas and are brushing your teeth as your mom calls you to say everyone else is ready to go. You hop in the car, and a few minutes later, you're pulling into the Star Dusk drive-in theater. Your father gets in line, is handed a piece of paper and grabs you a treat. As he pulls into a spot and makes sure the sound can be heard, your brother jumps into the back of the station wagon and you lie down on the back seat, just because you can. You kick off your slippers just as things start. You listen to a bit of music, and then the show begins with the preacher welcoming everyone before starting his message. Wait. What? Rewind. Preacher? Yes, this is the drive-in theater in 1954, and it's the Lake Street Methodist Sunday church service.

The Eau Claire Church began with meetings in worshippers' homes in 1857. By 1870, the congregation was large enough to construct a church building. The first structure was erected at the corner of Lake and Fourth Streets. In 1917, it was razed and rebuilt for $45,000. A new education wing was added in 1954.

That same year, Lake Street Methodist member Clare Brill mentioned that when he was in Florida for the winter, he attended a drive-in church service and that led to a new concept for Lake Street. The Stardusk, owned by the Grengs organization, agreed to make the theater available for no fee. Originally named Highway 53 Drive-In, the theater opened in 1949 with Robert Young in *Relentless* as its first film. Renamed Stardusk Drive-In a year later, it could accommodate 450 cars.

An organ and an altar were donated, and fresh flowers were furnished free of charge every week. Bulletins and refreshments, including rolls, donuts and coffee, were handed out. The first Sunday brought 259 people to the service.

The minister, Reverend M.O. Smith, was the first preacher at the drive-in. After the shorter service there at eight o'clock in the morning, Reverend Smith sped back to the church for his regularly scheduled indoor service at nine thirty. Some of his sermons were "The Freeway We Call Life," "The Man by the Side of the Road" and "The Strategy That Wins." Communion was held monthly, with "ushers" going car to car.

Surprisingly, the drive-in service was rarely canceled. The team had an elaborate tent system to protect people and equipment during stormy weather. The only real complaint was the noise when the Soo Line passed by.

According to church statistics, about 75 percent of the audience were Lake Street Methodist members, 20 percent were members of other local churches and 5 percent were travelers. When the offering was taken, several of the offering envelopes belonged to other churches. Lake Street was careful to separate them and pass them on to the appropriate congregation.

In 1965, Lake Street hired its first non-White minister, Reverend Perry Saito, and in 1979 its first female pastor, Linda Christman. While things might have been changing at the church building, at the drive-in, the only change was that cassette tapes provided the music in place of the organ.

Attendance remained steady. In 1967, the service averaged 240 people and 125 cars weekly. The highest recorded turnout was 357. In 1984, the Stardusk closed, and the church relocated to the Gemini Drive In, another Grengs theater property. One article mentioned that the drive-in was especially comfortable for handicapped individuals and young couples with babies.

When asked why they enjoyed this type of Sunday service, people shared some interesting responses:

"I like to get an early start on Sundays."

"I like outdoor services where we can hear the singing of birds, the wind, and even trucks and trains whizzing by."

"I prefer wearing pajamas to church."

"The short 45-min service appeals to me."

"I can control the speaker volume and even turn it off."

"I can lay down during the service and sleep if it's a boring one."

By 1988, attendance had declined. Most Sundays welcomed 115 to 120 people—decent numbers for a church service that began thirty-five years earlier.

It's the only church in town where you can come in your pajamas, with your golf clubs, your hair in curlers, and the smell of stink bait on your hands.

"No shoes, No shirt, No service" doesn't apply at Lake Street United Methodist Church's summer ministry at the Gemini Drive-in Theater. Because starting June 6, there will be a service every Sunday no matter how you choose to come. Barefoot. Riding bareback. Baring your soul. We really don't care, and we have a hunch the Lord doesn't either.

Now, that doesn't make worshipping with us at the drive-in any better than worshipping someplace else, but it does make it different. For one thing, you're in your car instead of a pew. For another, even if you're tone deaf, you can sing the hymns as loudly and boldly as you please without fear of disturbing the folks around you.

Other than that, the service is pretty much what you'd experience at our downtown church. Some special music. Reading the scripture. A sermon. A time to praise God. Gaining the sense or renewal and of strength that comes from being with the Lord in a Christian community. And the opportunity to thank God for making our Wisconsin summer weekends so special we just have to get out and enjoy them.

So, on your way to your summer fun, make your first stop a moment with the Lord. Services start this Sunday, June 6, at 8 a.m. At the Gemini Drive-In Theater on Highway 12 west (just east of its intersection with I-94).

Special note to those who have been worshiping with us at Lake Street North. You folks already know what it's like to worship in a non-traditional setting. So you won't have any problem moving to the drive-in for June, July and August. Services at our Folsom Street location will resume on the first Sunday in September.

Lake Street United Methodist Church

Downtown:
Corner of Lake Street and Fourth Avenue
Services at 9 & 10:30 a.m.

Gemini Drive-In:
Hwy. 12 West, just east of I35 & #12 intersection.
Service at 8 a.m.

Ad from the *Leader Telegram* for the Lake Street Methodist drive-in service, June 4, 1999. *Courtesy of the Leader Telegram.*

The Methodist drive-in era came to an end in 2010. When I asked current pastor Jerry Morris why the service was discontinued, he said that the primary reason for ending the decades of outdoor service was the shortage of volunteers to help haul items and set up at the drive-in. In 2020, when the COVID-19 pandemic hit, the church did not consider the drive-in option because services were available on the radio, YouTube and Facebook.

What a great "service," pun intended, for the church to provide to the city for so many years.

PART V

MINDING OUR OWN BUSINESS

Chapter 28
WINSLOW CAMP REMEDIES

by Jodi Kiffmeyer

By necessity, logging camps were usually located miles from any settlement. When a lumberjack got sick or injured, he couldn't just walk to the drugstore for medicine. Injuries were frequent and ranged from mild to severe. For example, on January 29, 1884, the *Eau Claire Leader* reported on seven recent admissions to the city hospital. Six of them were from the lumber camps. Their maladies included malaria, a lacerated knee, "dropsy" (swelling), a bruised back, a sprained knee and a broken jaw. A few years earlier, the *Leader* had reported on the toughness of one Oconto County lumberjack who, when his arm was severed by sleigh runners, "picked up his dismembered hand and walked to the camp, half a mile."

George F. Winslow, an Eau Claire pharmacist, saw the need for some kind of medical treatment at lumber camps and had an idea to meet it. Beginning in 1886, he put together medicine chests full of his own concoctions, called Winslow Camp Remedies, and shipped them to lumber camps in Wisconsin, Minnesota, Michigan's Upper Peninsula and as far away as Washington State (then still a territory).

Rumor has it Winslow's recipes were mostly alcohol. Though they could do nothing for an amputated limb, their contents brought some comfort to men suffering unimaginable injuries without the benefit of painkillers. No doubt they were popular in the "dry" logging camps for that reason. Lumberjacks consumed so many bottles of "Wonder Worker" and "Magic Bomb" that Winslow reported shipping twenty-five tons of medicine in

George Winslow at a lumber camp next to an advertisement for his remedies. *Courtesy Chippewa Valley Museum.*

1892. The feds caught on during Prohibition and arrested Winslow in 1922 for selling a patent medicine reported to contain 94 percent alcohol.

The income from his remedies, combined with the money he brought in from his downtown drug and wallpaper store near the Grand Avenue bridge, made Winslow a wealthy man. As evidence, check out the mansion he built in 1889, which still stands at 210 Oakwood Place. But perhaps the most fitting tribute to Mr. Winslow is the salutation from a letter addressed to him in 1891: "Sir George F. Winslow, designer, compounder and dispenser of concoctions for the alleviate [*sic*] of suffering among men and beasts while toiling among the pines."

Chapter 29

The Lady Embalmers

by Jodi Kiffmeyer

O n November 11, 1909, the *Eau Claire Leader* broke the news that Miss Bessie W. Miller died at Sacred Heart Hospital after a brief illness. The headline read "Lady Embalmer Passes Away." Less than a year earlier, in December 1908, the news had been brighter— she'd completed a course of study at Philadelphia Training School for Embalmers and successfully passed the state licensing exam "with very high markings." Her obituary included the astounding fact that nineteen-year-old Miss Miller had worked with R.H. Stokes, undertaker, since she was about fifteen years old.

The *Leader* assured readers that Bessie was "a young woman of keen intelligence, a ready wit and charming personality," maybe because many would think undertaking an odd or inappropriate occupation for a young woman. She was one of the only licensed lady embalmers in the area, but she wasn't the first in Eau Claire. As far as I can tell, that distinction belongs to Mrs. Ella Dean, who claimed to have secured the second undertaking license awarded to a woman in Wisconsin. By 1906, the *Leader* had crowned Ella the only female embalmer in the state.

Female undertakers were a necessity in a culture that didn't like to make exceptions to physical boundaries between genders and, as such, were often specifically advertised where they existed. Women had been doing the job for decades alongside their husbands, fathers and brothers, but around the turn of the twentieth century in Wisconsin, they had started to seek the recognition of state certification. In the case of Mrs. Dean, she and her husband, Sandy, had been caring for bodies from their funeral parlor at 342 Water Street since 1900.

Again, lest readers clutch at pearls, a *Leader* article described our lady embalmer in safe terms: "Mrs. Dean…is a comely lady, pleasant-voiced and mild-mannered, keenly alive to the humor of a good joke, and a most agreeable person to see and converse with." As further reassurance, Mrs. Dean herself added, "Of course…my work is confined exclusively to women and children." The only hint she might be frustrated by attitudes toward her gender came later in the interview. When asked by the reporter if she made night calls by herself, she replied, "To be sure…there is really nothing more to attending a night call than there is to a day visit, except the mere fact of it being dark." Perhaps the man assumed she was displaying her keen sense of humor. The modern reader detects a bit of a jab.

Chapter 30

Hey, Dude! Derge Cigars

by Diana Peterson

In 1951, Eau Claire said goodbye to one of its oldest residents: Dude Holzmann. Weighing in at 135 pounds, Dude was in pretty good shape, considering that he arrived in Eau Claire in 1875. Sure, he had some rot in his arm, a few fingers were missing and he suffered from a long crack in his back. However, with a few repairs, he was almost like new. Dude Holzmann was the statue that sat in front of the Derge Cigar Co.

In the early part of the century, it wasn't uncommon to go to a local store to buy cigars that had been made nearby. Julius Derge was a longtime cigar maker in the city.

Cigar makers typically started at the cigar companies as teenagers, cleaning the buildings and running errands. It could often take about three years to gain a spot on the factory floor. Workers weren't paid a lot of money, but they did make a decent living with little physical labor and normal hours. A hardworking employee could produce three hundred cigars a day and often earned about ten dollars for every thousand cigars he made. Factories were usually open six days a week and closed for lunch daily.

Julius was born in what is now Brandenburg, Germany, in 1853. He came to the United States with his brother in 1870 and learned the cigar-making business in Milwaukee before relocating to Eau Claire in 1875.

The company, J. Derge and Brother, was located at 124 South Barstow. When Julius's brother Ferdinand died, Julius's son Frank came on board. In 1898, the Derge Building was constructed at 12 South Barstow Street. Julius oversaw the manufacturing of cigars, and the company was in business for

Dude Holzman in front of the Derge Cigar Store, 12 South Barstow Street, circa 1900. *Courtesy Chippewa Valley Museum.*

seventy-two years. During that time, Julius made many improvements and received several patents for processing and storage technologies.

In 1908, Julius not only transferred Vuelta Abajo tobacco from Havana, Cuba, to Eau Claire, but he also hired several Cubans to relocate to Eau Claire to produce the cigars. In 1916, the firm became Madoro Cigar Co. There were branches in Racine, Stevens Point, Sheboygan and Chippewa Falls, as well as stands in the Eau Claire and Galloway hotels. At that time, twelve cigar makers were employed in the area, producing about fourteen thousand cigars a week. In 1947, the Derge cigar-making business was sold to John Bach, while the store continued.

John Bach came to Eau Claire in 1917 and apprenticed at Derge Cigar. In 1929, he decided to raise chickens. When that didn't work out, he opened his own cigar business in 1946. In 1947, Frank sold Bach the Derge equipment, and Bach continued to make cigars until he retired in 1959.

When the factory shut down, Frank continued to sell cigars and candies in the cigar store. Frank patented a beer stein container to store cigars during shipping. Because cedar was beginning to get scarce and expensive in the early 1900s, Frank designed a ceramic mug to reduce costs. The lining was moistureproof and dustproof to keep the cigars in perfect condition.

And once the cigars were removed, the customer had a new stein to use. Interestingly, several of his first orders came from Madison cigar stores who wanted a red *W* printed on them for their customers who attended the University of Wisconsin.

Both the store and the factory had the ubiquitous wooden sculpture in front of them. Beginning in the early 1800s, store owners displayed symbols to let customers know what they sold. For example, a red, white and blue pole symbolized a barbershop, while a mortar and pestle meant a drugstore. A Native American chief typically indicated a tobacco store. The use of wooden sculptures of Native Americans to symbolize tobacco stores originated in England when ships began bringing tobacco back from the Americas. Because many traders bought tobacco from Indigenous people, it made sense to use that symbol at the time.

Eventually, a wooden chief came to represent a quality cigar store. When sailing vessels were made obsolete by steamboats, a lot of artists who carved bowsprit figureheads lost their jobs. They began carving not only wooden Indians but also other figures. According to the Penn Museum, in the early 1900s, there were 100,000 wooden statues across the United States, but by the '50s, that number had been reduced to about 3,000, with 2,800 in private collections.

The Eau Claire cigar factory had a wooden statue that was referred to as "the dude," which Julius and Ferdinand had shipped from Germany when they came to Eau Claire. Julius called his statue Dude Holzmann, meaning "wooden man" in German. He wore a blue coat, gray trousers, an ecru hat and a maroon tie. In 1951, this dude was sold to a private collector in Pittsburg, Pennsylvania. Eau Claire was sad to see him go, but he had earned a quiet retirement.

Chapter 31

THIS JOB CLICKED WITH SOME PEOPLE

by Diana Peterson

In the early 1900s, the most common jobs were found in agriculture, manufacturing and domestic service. These jobs were all demanding physically and did not provide a substantial income. Most working women were relegated to domestic service, teaching or nursing. However, a new opportunity developed during the beginning of the twentieth century that changed the life of many young adults: telegraphy.

A telegrapher in that time could be compared to a software programmer today. This industry experienced rapid growth across the United States, creating demand for people with technical skills. To be accepted into telegraphy school, a candidate needed to be very literate, an excellent speller, capable of learning Morse code and knowledgeable about electricity.

Three telegraph schools existed in Wisconsin in the early 1900s: Northwestern Telegraph in Eau Claire, the Reidelback School of Telegraphy in La Crosse and the Valentine Telegraph School in Janesville.

Leonard Loken was born in 1880 in Eau Claire. He enlisted during the Spanish-American War in 1898, eventually landing in Puerto Rico, where he suffered from sunstroke. After his recovery, he studied telegraphy in Janesville, Wisconsin. After graduation, he went to work for the Omaha Railroad until 1909. In 1908, Union College started the Northwestern Telegraph School, and it transferred ownership of the school to Loken in early 1909.

Originally, only men were recruited. A 1909 ad in the *Leader Telegram* touted the "unlimited advantages offered to young men." However, the demand was so great that the industry began to change. The profession was

One of the graduating classes from Northwest Telegraph School, circa 1920. *Courtesy Chippewa Valley Museum.*

somewhat unique because women were well-represented in the field. They performed the same tasks as men, using the same equipment and working cooperatively together. And, significantly, women received the same wages as men. One of the instructors at the school was Miss Cornelia Malium.

Graduates were guaranteed a bright future, as the school promised that "the work is easy and pleasant, the pay good, and the opportunities for advancement unlimited." The Omaha Railroad had agreed to give Eau Claire graduates preferential consideration above other candidates. The railroad hired all nineteen graduates from the first class. One local veteran was interviewed in the paper about his recent hire as a telegrapher. He mentioned that it was a job he could do well with one arm and he was making $159 a month.

The school offered its students more than just technical skills. There was a men's baseball team and a women's softball team, both nicknamed the Clicks. The Lokens hosted events at their home at 618 Erin Street for the students, including a Valentine's party in 1912 and a social night honoring Cornelia Malium.

The school also held dances for its students. In 1914, one hundred people gathered in Laycock Hall. Leonard announced beforehand that there was to be absolutely no tango dancing! Waltzes, two-steps and quadrilles were allowed. The music was furnished by Sherman's Orchestra. Fred Nerbonne called the square dance numbers. "Mrs. George Hagen and Mrs. Leonard Loken provided the supper. The dancing continued until very late, and no one left until the last dance."

In the mid-1920s, there were some indications that life in telegraphy was changing. In 1927, the Associated Press installed two automatic printer telegraph machines, which took the place of human telegraphers. Loken realized that the profession might be declining. In June that same year, Governor Zimmerman appointed Loken register of deeds on the death of Anton Anderson, and the school closed.

Chapter 32

LIGHTS! CAMERA! ACTION!

by Diana Peterson

In 1933, Hollywood came to Eau Claire with a world premiere of the movie *Out All Night*, a comedy starring ZaSu Pitts and Slim Summerville. It was shown at the State Theater at 11:30 p.m. on April 8.

Giant searchlights, flares and streamers reminded the city of the film's arrival. The high school drama class interacted with patrons, impersonating famous stars. Dick Bradley of the State Theater said it was the first time Eau Claire had the honor of hosting the world premiere of a movie.

The plot of the movie is a typical one for the 1930s. Ronald Colgate (Summerville), a shy guy who lives with his mother (played by Laura Hope Crews), meets Bonny (Pitts) and falls in love. Billy Barty and Shirley Temple are also in the cast. The distributor was Universal Pictures. Movies were a little shorter at that time, and this one came in at sixty-eight minutes. The official release dates were April 8 and 13, 1933.

The big question this film asked was: "Will apron strings loosen or tighten when social introverts consider love and marriage in *Out All Night?*" Widow Jane Colgate convinces her son he is suffering from various illnesses and must be extra careful. One day, they go to Stacey's Department Store to buy a coat, and he wanders into the store nursery, meets Bonny, a nurse, and falls in love. After he gets up enough courage to ask Bonny on a date, his mother insists on chaperoning the couple. When the couple gets locked in the store overnight, Ronald proposes to Bonny. On the train to their honeymoon, there's a mix-up, and Ronald goes to the wrong room. Back in New York, Bonny asks for a divorce, thinking her husband cheated on her. After several

The Wurlitzer Opus 1204 organ at the State Theater, 1929. *Courtesy Chippewa Valley Museum.*

more mishaps, the couple reconciles and gets their honeymoon after all. The film's working title was *Niagara Falls*.

The State Theater opened in 1926 as a vaudeville house, and the last shows there were movies. The 1,300-seat theater was built by Finkelstein and Ruben out of Minnesota for $315,000 (more than $5 million in today's dollars). Finkelstein and Ruben operated theaters in Wisconsin, Minnesota and North and South Dakota. They brought the experts in to add the finishing touches. Universal Scenic Co. came in to arrange the lighting. Painter Carl Olson, trained under European artists, created wall murals. W.R. Gallagher, who was one of the top organ installers, set up the Wurlitzer organ. This instrument was one of the most talked-about topics in Eau Claire at the time; it had a price tag of $20,000. The average theater owner would never even consider including a Wurlitzer because they were so expensive. A *Leader Telegram* article from December 30, 1925, mentioned that the organ "was equivalent to a 35-piece orchestra" and it "had ten miles of electric cables and 13,000 electrical connections."

The cost of a movie ticket was forty cents for evening shows and twenty-five for matinees, with a discounted rate of ten cents for kids.

The opening of the theater had to compete with a storm. The evening's entertainment included the Orpheus overture under conductor Mike Degelman, a newsreel, a comedy, a jazz revue, a performance with eighteen singers and dancers, a novelty film and the silent feature *Classified* with Corinne Griffith. The theater received congratulatory telegrams from Douglas Fairbanks, Mary Pickford, Charles Chaplin and Harold Lloyd.

One person who most likely was in the audience that night was Mary Ritzinger. For fifty years, her family home stood on the lot where the theater was built, and she received a free pass for 1926.

By 1928, talking pictures had started taking over the industry. *The Jazz Singer* is often mentioned as the first talking film, but it was only partially a talkie, while *The Lights of New York* with Helene Costello was the first all-talking picture. Both movies were seen and heard at the State that year.

The basement of the theater was also a fun place, with eight bowling alleys, a pool table, billiards and snooker. A dance hall occupied the second floor.

In addition to the shows at the theater, radio station WTAQ hosted a dinner concert from the theater every Monday, Wednesday and Thursday. From five thirty to six thirty, Obbie Erickson played dining music. Requests could be mailed directly to the theater. He also did a special performance from eleven o'clock to midnight on Wednesdays. The last audience of the day was invited to stay for it.

One of the theater's icons was John Stubbs. Stubbs began working in local theaters selling popcorn at age fourteen. The popcorn was made at another site, and the vendors had to retrieve it and sell it walking up and down the aisles. He received his projectionist union card at age eighteen, in 1925.

When the State opened, Stubbs was hired as a stage electrician. He worked with the vaudeville circuit for a few years. While he worked for other theaters occasionally, he was employed by the State for forty-five of the fifty-seven years that he worked in the industry. He recalled some of the new techniques that had been introduced over the years, including Technicolor; Cinemascope, which featured wider images; and 3D films, which often gave people headaches and never seemed to work properly.

In 1937, major renovations occurred at the State. The *Leader Telegram* described the "beautiful foyer and lobby, the magic fountain, pillars of light, exquisite drapes, plush carpets, new stage sets, indirect lighting fixtures, and updated décor."

In addition to the movies, there were a lot of special events at the State. Cooperative Thanksgiving services were held there, with Obbie Erickson playing the hymns. The theater hosted Christmas parties for kids, baby contests, war bond sales and special acting opportunities for locals.

Sadly, in 1973, the Wurlitzer pipe organ was removed. The State showcased some of Hollywood's most legendary films, including *Doctor Zhivago*, *Jaws* and *Star Wars*. By 1982, single-screen theaters were no longer profitable, and the last movie was shown at the State that year. The theater was sold as a venue for live performances. But many memories of the opulent theater remain in the stories of residents who fondly recall special nights at this charming location. The Eau Claire Regional Arts Council asked locals who spent time at the State to share some of their favorite moments at the theater. The stories detailed first dates and first kisses, sneaking cigarettes in the men's room and catching two movies for the price of one because the theater wasn't cleared out between films.

Chapter 33

A House Ahead of Its Time

by Diana Peterson

After World War II, soldiers coming home to Eau Claire dreamed of having a family and a suburban home. What they found was a housing crisis. Eau Claire was literally out of homes, as were many other cities. A few solutions were found to ensure that families had a place to live.

In September 1945, Eau Claire asked the National Housing Agency for two hundred demountable houses. These houses were built of plywood in units. One section was a combination kitchen/living room, and the others were bedrooms. Each home came with an electric hot plate, a hot water heater, a shower/bath and a refrigerator.

The city was required to pay part of the cost for shipping the homes, which came two to a truck. The city also had to provide lots with temporary streets, as well as water and sewer services. The cities using the homes were not allowed to make a profit renting them, and they had to be returned to the government when they were no longer in use.

Eau Claire made the homes available to any family with at least one ex–service member. In October 1945, one hundred of these homes were transported from the Badger Ordnance Plant in Merrimac to the Drummond Packing Co. property on both sides of Birch Street. By December 1945, 320 families had put in a request for one of the homes, so the city applied for another round of temporary houses.

In 1946, houses were built at an astounding rate, but there were not enough homes to keep up with the demand. The Lustron Company developed an all-steel, prefabricated, bungalow-style home to speed up production.

The Lustron homes were constructed of enameled steel panels. The design was the brainchild of Carl Strandlund, a Swedish immigrant. Strandlund had been a vice president and general manager of the Chicago Vitreous Enamel Co. in Cicero, Illinois. They made the exterior panels for gas stations and restaurants.

Strandlund hired architects Roy Burton Blass and Morris H. Beckman to sketch out some ideas for these new homes. He received a $12.5-million-dollar loan from the federal government through the Reconstruction Finance Corporation to fabricate the panels and set up shop in a former war plane manufacturing plant in Columbus, Ohio. A lot of the employees were veterans.

The steel walls and roof of the homes had a baked enamel finish on the exterior and interior that made them almost maintenance-free. Permanent fireproof insulation and a specially designed radiant panel heating system ensured that the homes were inexpensive to heat. An oil-fired air furnace heated the metal ceiling tiles. The exterior of the home could be cleaned with a hose. A Lustron brochure summarized the ease of caring for the home: "The all-steel construction makes the Lustron home completely termite proof, vermin proof, and rat proof. It's also fire-proof, decay proof, stain proof, saltwater proof—let's say it's almost maintenance proof."

Purchasers had the choice of eight models in surf blue, maize yellow, desert tan or dove gray. The bathrooms featured built-in vanities, the bedrooms had pocket doors and the kitchen included a built-in under-the-sink Thor washing machine that could be turned into a dishwasher by adding a dish rack.

Advertisements let families know that "what Lustron offers is a new way of life." The homes cost $6,000 to $10,000 each; every home required twelve tons of steel and one ton of enamel. Each house was delivered in 3,300 parts by Lustron employees, who assembled it on top of a concrete slab in about 350 hours.

The first homes came off the production line in 1949. The houses were selling quickly, and Strandlund tried to keep up with the demand. By 1950, Lustron had manufactured 2,680 homes—but they had promised 45,000. The company was unable to contain costs enough to earn a profit. To make money, the company needed to produce 50 homes per day, but it was averaging 26.

In 1950, an investigation by the Senate Banking Committee uncovered a corruption scandal within the company. The loan was called in, and the company was forced into bankruptcy. However, many businessmen said that

The Emma Julin home on Fairway Street, 2024. *Courtesy Diana Peterson.*

the corruption story was made up. Lustron was constantly under attack from lobbyists and construction syndicates that opposed its efficiency in building.

St. Louis resident Tom Bakersmith, a Lustron historian, says that in one sense, the homes were made too well. It's hard to find material for repairs today. Lustron owners scramble to find solutions for replacement parts. This lack of parts has led to many homes being demolished.

About 1,500 Lustron homes still exist. Eau Claire has three of them. A surf blue house is at 1831 Badger Avenue, and a maize yellow one is at 1819 Lyndale. The maize yellow home on Fairway Street, the Emma Julin House, is the only one to feature a garage. It was designated an Eau Claire Landmark because of its unique construction.

Eighty years later, these prefabricated houses are still almost maintenance-free. Hopefully, Eau Claire's collection of Lustrons will continue to be preserved.

Chapter 34

CAN IT: GERMAN POW CAMPS IN EAU CLAIRE

by Diana Peterson

I f you were a fan of *Hogan's Heroes*, you might have wondered where a mirror image of the show about German POWs in the United States might be set. If you thought Eau Claire might be a good location, you would be right.

In 1942, the British requested that the United States take Axis prisoners to avoid the Nazis air-dropping weapons into England's prison camps. From 1942 to 1945, more than four hundred thousand POWs were brought to American soil. Wisconsin had twenty thousand captured enemy soldiers in thirty-eight different camps, the largest being Fort McCoy.

In July 1945, Kenneth Lange, president of Lange Canning, said that sixty Jamaicans had arrived in Eau Claire to work for the company and that prisoners of war were on the way. He emphasized that even with those additional workers, "there will still be a shortage of manpower in the pea fields, at the viners, and at the plant." He assured the public that "German war prisoners will be used only as long as there is a lack or shortage of civilian labor."

Eau Claire found the perfect POW camp. In 1941, the 4-H fairgrounds had been built. There were two dormitories, each furnished with bunk beds and a kitchen. An area plumbed for water where livestock were washed before shows easily became a communal shower once tents were put up around it. With the addition of a wire fence and two guard towers, it became a POW camp.

In all, 175 POWs were brought to Eau Claire. The camp was run by the U.S. Army, with Captain Hodges in charge. One group harvested peas and left in time for the August fair to set up. A second group was brought in September to pick corn.

With so many young men entering the war, Wisconsin was left with a shortage of labor on farms. According to a *USA* article from April 2019 ("Just Like Us: How Wisconsin Held Captive, and Made Peace with, German POWs in WWII," by Sarah Razner), "About 13,000 POWs were placed at 38 makeshift camps located from as far north as Bayfield to as far south as Janesville. They set to work harvesting potatoes, corn, apples, cherries and sugar beets—a critical commodity used for making the industrial alcohol needed to manufacture munitions and synthetic rubber." The *Leader Telegram* reported that without these prisoners of war, many of the fruit and vegetable crops in Wisconsin would have been lost from 1942 to 1945.

Many Wisconsinites connected with these prisoners. One third of the state's population was of German descent and many had family members who still spoke German at home. The prisoners worked side by side with families and farm employees to harvest crops. Many American workers soon came to understand that the German POWs were not Nazis, just young boys who were drafted into fighting for Hitler's reign of terror. Farm wives often

Lange Canning, where German POWs worked in 1945. *Courtesy Chippewa Valley Museum.*

made them pies and other treats. Residents enjoyed sitting along Highway 53 to watch them play soccer where the Eastridge parking lot is today.

Few escapes were reported. Typically, if someone did sneak off, it was on an adventure searching for women or beer.

In the *USA* article, Gerhard Pechmann, a Madison resident, is quoted talking about his father's time in Wisconsin. His dad, Kurt, was taken into the German military as a teen and was a POW in Wisconsin from ages twenty-one to twenty-three. He said that "most guards treated the POWs like human beings. Many who took the job were farmers or GIs who'd been injured in war."

Pechmann recalled stories his father shared of "POWs waking the guard when the commander popped in for a surprise inspection, and guards giving POWs their rifles for target practice. The men were allowed to form soccer teams within the camps and in Hartford the POWs watched films— at first propaganda, but later popular movies starring Shirley Temple and Roy Rogers."

Many prisoners maintained close relationships with Eau Claire citizens and continued to write to them after the war ended. Several prisoners returned to the United States to live after spending time there. In 2019, Marge Lind of Wisconsin described some of these interactions. "They were just teenage boys, nice kids that my mother baked bread for," recalls the eighty-seven-year-old Lind. "For years my folks got letters from some of the boys after they returned home. There was that kind of a connection."

Although these young Germans were brought to Eau Claire to help harvest crops, perhaps the most important thing they harvested was the understanding that the "enemy" included young boys who were more alike than different from our local soldiers sent off to fight in a foreign land. Residents treated them with the same kindness they hoped German mothers might show to their sons. As Abraham Lincoln so wisely said, "Do I not destroy my enemies when I make them my friends?"

Chapter 35
INTEGRATING BASEBALL IN EAU CLAIRE

by Jodi Kiffmeyer

I t's hard to find anyone who's lived in Eau Claire for any length of time who doesn't know about Hank Aaron's connection to the city. He played for Eau Claire's minor league team, the Bears, in 1952 before moving to the big leagues with the Milwaukee Braves. Hammerin' Hank was one of the earliest Black baseball players in Eau Claire, but the first two beat him by a couple years.

The first glimpse Eau Claire residents had of Bill Bruton and Roy White was a photo published in the April 27, 1950 edition of the *Eau Claire Leader*. A large caption under the photo read "First Colored Bears," just in case it wasn't obvious to readers. The local Toastmasters club—an organization meant to help members improve leadership and speaking skills—met at the end of March that year and discussed the topic of integrating baseball. Rumors had reached the city that the Bears were going to bring Black players into town. Near the end of the meeting, members took a vote and decided "Eau Claire is not a suitable city for a Negro baseball player."

Over the next couple months, readers registered their opinions on the matter in letters to the *Leader*'s editor. There's a good chance Bruton and White read some of them after they arrived in Eau Claire. If so, they would have learned that one businessman didn't want them in his restaurant because they probably didn't know how to behave and might become too familiar with White women. A week later, another reader said intermarriage was the only solution for racism, so it was a mixed bag. Most letters were in favor of integrating Eau Claire baseball. The *Eau Clarion*, a picture magazine published in Eau Claire for less than a year, printed photos of the men, just below the words "We Welcome" in bold print.

Bill Bruton ended up in the major leagues, playing first for the Milwaukee Braves and ending his career with the Detroit Tigers. Born in Panola, Alabama, in 1925, Bruton had little opportunity to play baseball in a formal setting. His school had no team, and segregation kept him away from everything but the neighborhood sandlot. However, he did have the chance to attend games played by the Birmingham Black Barons, one of the first eight Negro League teams organized in 1920. After graduating high school, Bruton volunteered for the army, serving from 1944 to 1947.

On returning from overseas service, Bruton moved north and began moving up the ranks in baseball. He started out in the Negro Leagues with the Philadelphia Stars. In 1950, he caught the eye of a Boston Braves scout, who recruited Bruton and sent him to Eau Claire to gain skills playing for the Bears.

As a professional player, Bruton was known for his speed and, later, for his part in encouraging Major League Baseball to finish the integration process it started with Jackie Robinson in 1947. Although players could mix on the field, in many cities and almost all ball clubs they were still separated by race in housing, on transportation and at meals. Their families were segregated while cheering in the stands. Beginning in 1961, Bruton challenged reluctant owners of Major League Baseball teams to put an end to segregation of players in southern cities where teams held spring training. His philosophy: "As important as a ball club is to these cities…it can have a lot to say about housing if it wants to." Within two years, Bruton's efforts paid off. In 1963, the Detroit Tigers were the last team to integrate. Ironically, Bruton was playing for them at the time.

Until recently, I knew very little about Roy White. He doesn't appear in the museum's copy of the 1952 official team photo and never made it to the pros. But in the spring of 2023, I got a visit from Maureen Slauson, daughter of a former Catholic high school football coach and English teacher, Marty Crowe. According to Maureen, when the Bears were searching for lodging in 1950, every prospective home for the two Black players seemed to evaporate. The team secretary remembered that Marty Crowe rented rooms to help pay the bills and asked if he had space for four ball players. "Send them over," Crowe said. "Two of them are Black," was the reply. Marty simply repeated, "Send them over."

Maureen brought me some manuscripts and newspaper articles her dad wrote. To my delight, one of them was entirely about Roy White. It had

Bill Bruton. *Courtesy Chippewa Valley Museum.*

enough detail that I was able to find his obituary and other sources that filled out the story of his life a bit. What follows is a short eulogy I wrote for the museum's social media accounts:

Roy was born on August 15, 1927, to Malcolm and Elvira White, who were renting a farm west of San Antonio. By March 1950, when the Milwaukee Braves reported for spring training in Austin, Texas, White was

Roy White. *Courtesy Chippewa Valley Museum.*

playing for the city's Black Pioneers, a Negro League team. His pitching caught the eye of scouts, who sent him to Eau Claire for "seasoning" in the minor leagues. White was quieter, darker-skinned and less charismatic than Bruton. According to Marty Crowe, who rented a room to both men, White seemed to struggle with loneliness and isolation. He injured his arm early in the season, and the Bears let him go before the 1950 official team photo was taken.

After leaving Eau Claire, Roy served in the U.S. Army and continued working as a senior clerk at Fort Sam Houston Army Post when he'd completed his time in the military. He married his wife, Claudia, in 1950, and the couple went on to have one son and several grandchildren and great-grandchildren. He died on July 2, 2019, at the age of ninety-one.

It's inevitable and appropriate that Hank Aaron is remembered as a highlight of Eau Claire's baseball history. Let's invite the barrier-breaking duo of Bill Bruton and Roy White to join him in the city's memory.

Chapter 36

I Can't Believe It's Butter

by Diana Peterson

Wisconsin is the Dairy State, and butter is one of its most important products. The John Wuethrich family arrived from Switzerland in 1893 and started a butter business. In 1911, the family purchased the company that would become Grassland Dairy. Five generations later, they are still producing butter in Wisconsin.

In 1970, the dairy started experimenting with various butter products. A rabbi was hired to supervise the production of kosher butter for Passover. This was the only creamery in Wisconsin providing the product; about 125,000 pounds were made during the four-day process.

That same year, the dairy introduced a new butter product: Mountain Meadow, flavored butter. It was produced in a variety of flavors: honey, cinnamon, garlic, maple, clove, chocolate and orange. The butter was marketed for use on bread, pancakes and vegetables. It was made with only natural flavors: oranges and chives from California, maple syrup and honey from Wisconsin and real chocolate, garlic and cinnamon. The product had a test run in Milwaukee, and the flavored butters proved so popular that they were released into the Eau Claire and Merrill-Rhinelander areas. Ads for local grocery stores featured $0.10 off coupons.

The *Wall Street Journal* published an article about the butters, and Grassland was flooded with phone calls from people around the country who wanted to know more. One of those calls came from Helen Marcus with the national game show *What's My Line?* Helen was a casting director who worked for both *What's My Line?* and *To Tell the Truth*.

Brothers John D. (*left*) and L. Allen (*right*) Weutrich showing off the Mountain Meadow line of flavored butter products, 1970. *Courtesy Grassland Dairy.*

What's My Line? debuted in 1950, and the weekly scheduled show went off the air in 1967. It was produced by the well-known team of Mark Goodson and Bill Todman. For most of its life, the game show aired on Sunday nights. Four celebrity panelists asked contestants yes-or-no questions to try to determine their occupation. Whenever the contestants answered no to a question, the emcee flipped a card, and when ten cards had been flipped, the guest won fifty dollars.

The most famous panelists were Arlene Francis, Bennett Cerf and Dorothy Kilgallen. John Daly was the moderator. Viewers enjoyed their banter and sophisticated humor, as well as the glamorous clothing the panelists wore and the elegant atmosphere that surrounded the show. Watching it was like eavesdropping on a celebrity dinner party. The show won Emmys for Best Quiz or Audience Participation Show in 1952, 1953 and 1958.

Fun fact: the phrase "Is it bigger than a breadbox?" came from this show. Steve Allen asked the question in 1953, and it became a standard one after that episode.

Game shows were profitable to produce because their production costs were low. However, in 1967, CBS decided that game shows were no longer suitable for prime-time schedules and canceled several of them, including *What's My Line?* The series then went into syndication from 1967 until 1974.

When Marcus asked if someone from Grassland Dairy would appear on the show, Rolf Christophersen, their national sales manager, was chosen for the job. Christophersen lived on Fillmore Avenue in Eau Claire. The taping was done at the Ed Sullivan Theater in New York on December 3, 1970. The panelists that night were Arlene Francis, Anita Gillette, Robert Morse and Soupy Sales. Wally Brunner was the moderator. Appearing on the show with Christophersen were a physical fitness expert and celebrity guest Garry Moore. Right before the buzzer went off, Francis guessed his occupation had to do with butter. Christophersen provided the panelists with samples before he left the set.

Christophersen was born in 1915 in Pigeon Falls, Wisconsin. After graduating from Decorah College in Iowa, he joined the military during World War II, serving in Europe with Naval Intelligence. After his discharge, he went to work for Grassland Dairy. In 1968, he married widow Helen (Stark) Airis. The couple ran Christophersen's Collectibles for years. Helen passed away in 1968 and Rolf in 1999. Their collections were sold at auction in 2000.

I like to imagine Rolf, as an older gentleman, sharing the story of appearing on *What's My Line?* with his friends and family, tossing in a little bit of embellishment about his encounters with the stars.

And how long did the flavored butter last? Unfortunately, it was shut down almost immediately. Trevor J. Wuethrich, president of Grassland Dairy, said the company learned that many people bought it, used it once or twice and then forgot it was in the refrigerator or used it so sporadically that before they'd used most of it, it was no longer any good. That's too bad, because more than fifty years later, it still sounds like a great idea.

Chapter 37

WHO KNEW?

by Diana Peterson

Sometimes a headline jumps out at you and catches you by surprise and you have no choice but to take a minute to check it out. This chapter features a few of those can't-miss stories whose headlines drew my attention.

CAN'T FIND IT

DID ANYONE SEE A STRAY METEOR LYING AROUND LOOSE IN NORTHERN WISCONSIN?

In April 1908, a new gathering spot was created in Eau Claire. It wasn't a diner, park or tavern, although a few people suspected some citizens had been drinking when they first heard the news. A brilliant ball of fire fell from the sky and landed in Eau Claire near the Omaha train yards on Saturday, April 18, 1908. Luckily, the respectable Dr. Chase was one of the witnesses.

By the next day, sightings of the meteor had been reported by many across the state. Residents of La Crosse, Viroqua and Madison all watched it travel across the sky. The *Leader* reported that "the awesome visitor created considerable excitement" throughout the state. Professor Merrill told the *Leader* that he had received a letter about the meteor from weather bureau officials in Washington, D.C., who said it had an unusual brilliancy.

In fact, they mentioned that it was the most brilliant meteor they had ever recorded.

When it hit the ground, the meteor appeared to spread out in all directions. The *Leader Telegram* reported that the spot where the meteor landed was "plainly visible, but no one yet has found any portion of it, it being buried so deep in the ground."

This was not too surprising. The article also discussed a meteor that landed in Oregon a few months before. The residents who saw it land on a farm went to dig it out the next day. They finally found it buried one hundred feet in the earth. It was still red-hot, and it had to cool down for a month before it could be handled by humans. It was described as metallic black, about the size of a small backyard shed.

The newspaper concluded that "though science explains the meteor, there is something awesome in a visitation by one of these strange bodies, coming from nowhere and carrying—so far as humanity is concerned— no message." As a reminder, readers were told that "anyone finding the meteor in this section of the state to please bring it to the Lost and Found department of the *Leader*."

Teenage Girls Turn Up Here After Night Out

On June 11, 1955, a trio of Milwaukee girls gave themselves up to Eau Claire authorities.

Earlier in the week, the three girls (one sixteen and two fifteen years old) had stayed the night in a model home in Milwaukee without their parents' knowledge or permission. Apparently, the parents reported them missing, and when the girls arrived home the next day, one mother called the police to say they had returned. The police chief said her daughter should come down to the police station in the afternoon to give a statement.

Instead, the girl called her friends, and together they came up with thirty-three dollars and hopped on a bus to Eau Claire. On Wednesday night, they got a room at the Inn Hotel, but realizing they only had so much money, they went to Mrs. Alvin J. Lynnes's boardinghouse at 1616 Emery Street for Thursday night.

On Thursday, the girls wandered around the city, taking in a movie that evening. Perhaps they saw *Love Me or Leave Me* with Doris Day and James Cagney, which was playing at the State Theater. *Soldier of Fortune* with Clark Gable and Susan Hayward was showing at the Hollywood. They ate a meal downtown. At the Colonial Grille, they could have ordered a cheeseburger or an egg salad sandwich for $.30 or splurged for a hot beef sandwich with potatoes for $.60.

After spending some time sitting under the Water Street Bridge on Friday, they spotted the woods behind the State Teachers College and realized that could be a place for them to sleep at no cost. I'm not sure when it started to sink in that they were not safe in the woods or that their money was quickly running out, but sometime the next day, they turned themselves in, and their parents were allowed to pick them up on Sunday.

CAROLS TOO NOISY

To get shoppers in the Christmas spirit in 1953, Eau Claire began playing music from loudspeakers downtown. Christmas carols began the second week of December. On December 11, a caller phoned the police to complain about the loudness. He said the carols were now just noisy nuisances, especially when the "vibrant sounds rattle things on the desk during office hours." He said that he was trying not to be a Scrooge, but the carols were not bringing harmony. "They just about blast us out of the building. After a while it just becomes noise."

Because the man complained on a Friday, there was no time to take care of the problem until the next week, and Ken Esslinger from the chamber of commerce could not be reached for comment. The chamber arranged for the speakers to be turned on and the volume set.

I'm guessing the only song the businessman was looking forward to was "Silent Night."

RADIO STATIC EXPERTS OPEN PROBE HERE

On July 11, 1930, Eau Claire was under investigation. No, it wasn't a murder, government bribery or concealing water test results. L.M. Park, detective, arrived from Minneapolis to begin hunting for clues to clean up Eau Claire. You see, Park was a radio interference detective, and he was there to hunt down sources of static.

Radio distributors in the area were getting a lot of complaints from their customers about the static, so they undertook a campaign to deal with the problem. Park let no moss grow under his feet. By the next day, he was ready with a partial report. Both Western Union Telegraph and Wisconsin Telephone had agreed to patch lines that were causing problems. The local hospitals all agreed to rectify issues that their X-ray and diathermy machines were causing. (Diathermy machines use an electric current to stimulate heat generation deep within tissues.)

Park was getting ready to meet with Northern States Power because he had determined one of the biggest sources of static was the city's trolleys. He also mentioned that all the doctors' and dentists' offices could expect a visit from him, as well as several larger businesses.

I'm guessing Eau Claire residents slept much better that night knowing that soon, whether they were tuning into *The Lone Ranger*, *The Jack Benny Show* or *Dragnet*, they would have lines free and clear again.

Clothes Make a Difference All Right: Cowboy Garb of Visitor Brings Three Cops

Tourism was an important industry for Eau Claire in the 1930s, but apparently not all residents received the message. According to the *Leader Telegram*, a young adult visitor to the area "expressed his opinion that just because a man does not care to affect the common clothes worn by the average male today, is no reason why police should regard him as a suspicious character." I can't say that I see any reason to disagree with him.

On July 13, 1935, this young visitor was at the end of Newton Street at a vantage point overlooking the city. He was meeting a friend who was going to show him around town. Suddenly, he turned to see three armed policemen surrounding him. He said that he almost had a heart attack.

Apparently, one of the neighbors had thought he seemed dangerous and called the police. The young man was wearing cowboy trousers, a wide leather belt, a bright blue shirt and a black hat.

What I find most astounding about this story is that the same year it took place, one of the most popular movies was *Tumbling Tumbleweeds* with Gene Autry. One of the best-selling books was Zane Grey's *Code of the West*. D.J. O'Malley, "Cowboy Poet," was returning to Eau Claire for a performance. The Montana Cowboys were appearing at Fournier's. And Sears Roebuck and Co. took out an ad in the *Leader Telegram* for a seven-piece cowboy suit for $1.89. All I can say is, "Go West, young man. Go West."

Secret Basement, Tunnel Are Discovered in Ruins of Old Brewery Building

On May 4, 1932, the *Leader Telegram* reported that workers demolishing the Edward R. Hantzsch brewery had discovered a secret basement and attached tunnel. Hantzsch had arrived in the area in 1862. A former Prussian army officer, he was put in charge of a group of volunteer fighters in the area in case there were problems with local Indigenous people. There were not. Hantzsch decided to settle in Eau Claire and built a brewery at 413 South River Street (Graham Avenue).

Decades later, the workers demolishing the brewery discovered a secret basement room twenty feet long and six feet wide; it was separated from the building by a sixteen-foot solid stone wall. That room opened onto a secret tunnel that made its way to the Platner Building at 412 Barstow Street.

Old-timers claimed that it was a secret room because Hantzsch had legally brewed beer but illegally brewed whiskey. A few hours later, a network of lead pipes like those used for whiskey distillation were found leading to the room as well.

I guess Hantzsch was open to brewing beer, but when it came to whiskey, he had tunnel vision.

Cat Removed from Tree by City Fireman

I was wondering if one of those stories you hear on sitcoms about firemen rescuing cats from trees had ever happened in Eau Claire when the above headline caught my eye. In this case, in January 1938, a cat was up in a tree at the corner of Randall and Mappa Streets. Neighbors said it had been there for several days. So in between answering calls to five chimney fires, local firemen stopped by and retrieved the cat from the tree.

I did a little looking to see if there were more stories about firemen rescuers. I found another one from August 1938 where firemen helped remove a cat and mentioned that they got these calls throughout the year—and typically only got scratches for their rewards.

In September 1940, the *Leader Telegram* reported that there were no serious Labor Day happenings in the city, but firemen did have to rescue a cat from a tree.

I should have stopped my search after three, content and able to feel warm and fuzzy about our city's response to helping pets. Alas, I found one more story from June 1951 that revealed that Eau Claire had finally succumbed to red tape and "it's not my problem" logic.

Several residents called police to mention that their neighbor's cat was stuck up in a tree and meowing quite loudly. The police indicated that they had no equipment to help the cat and the firemen should be called. The firemen, not wanting their expensive equipment tied up with a cat if there was a fire alarm, referred the residents back to the police. The police phoned the county humane officer, who informed them that his duties did not include climbing trees after cats. Finally, the police thought of Joseph Beck, dog warden. Beck, who had a wooden leg, was not about to climb a tree, but he wanted to help, so he showed up—with a shotgun. If the cat seemed loud, that was nothing compared to the local housewives who chased Beck away with a barrage of insults. A few minutes later, Michael Prock Jr. arrived and quietly set up a ladder; retrieved the one-year-old cat, Ramsey; and returned it to little Pauline Knutson of 420 Seaver Street. Every neighborhood needs a Michael Prock Jr.

About the Authors

Jodi Kiffmeyer is the archivist at the Chippewa Valley Museum and a lifelong student of history. She grew up in Chetek, Wisconsin, and has lived in the Chippewa Valley for most of her life.

Diana Peterson arrived at the University of Wisconsin–Eau Claire in 1985 and never left. She is editor/assistant curator at the Chippewa Valley Museum, where she discovers and shares Eau Claire's stories.

Visit us at
www.historypress.com